DISCOVER THE POWER IN THE PRAYERS OF PAUL

by
David Bordon
with Rick Killian

Harrison House Publishers
Tulsa, Oklahoma

Manuscript prepared by Rick Killian, Killian Creative, Boulder, Colorado.
www.killiancreative.com
Editorial: SnapdragonGroup Editorial Services

09 08 07 06 05   10 9 8 7 6 5 4 3 2 1

Discover the Power in the Prayers of Paul
Copyright © 2005 by Harrison House, Inc.
ISBN 1-57794-735-5

Published by Harrison House, Inc.
P.O. Box 35035
Tulsa, Oklahoma 74135

CONTENTS

PART 2: *Praying the Prayers of Paul*

PREFACE

The apostle Paul was a man of prayer.

More than any of the first apostles, he had to be. He had not walked with Jesus as the twelve had. He did not have opportunity to see Jesus reach out His hand to heal or hear Him teach with authority, or see Him minister day in and day out, seven days a week, twenty-four hours a day. Those who walked with Jesus for three years had a tangible relationship with Him, memories to look back on. They had seen miracles and witnessed Jesus' grace and courage on the Cross. They had heard His comforting words and stood watching as their Lord Jesus was caught up into the heavens. But Paul did not. If Paul was going to know Jesus intimately, he would have to meet Him in prayer. What the others had experienced in the natural, Paul had access to only in the Spirit. We learn about the life of Jesus through the accounts of the gospel writers, but Paul's writing teaches us to love a God we cannot see or touch. From him, we learn how to be led by the Holy Spirit.

The depth of Paul's letters to the churches reveals that his prayer life was rich and rewarding. Through his time waiting on God, Paul received revelation and instruction for living the new life Jesus died and rose again to bring us—a life no longer dictated by legalistic interpretations of God's written Word, a life lived by the power of the Holy Spirit.

Paul's writings make up more than two-thirds of the New Testament. While his teachings provide the "how to" and "what to do" of the Christian life, it is his prayers that reveal and call for the "spiritual power" that make you able "to do the right thing" in any and every given circumstance. It is one thing to understand living by the law of love, as Jesus proclaimed, but it is quite another to have the inner strength to do it day in and day out in a world motivated mostly by self-centeredness and personal hurts. Paul's prayers reveal the spiritual strengths and assets you need to act out divine love in all situations.

Yet Paul's prayers are special for yet another reason. Inspired by the Holy Spirit, they literally have the power to help you affirm and boldly confess who you are in Christ. When you pray the prayers of Paul, you are praying God's Word—which is His will—into your life and the lives of others. By their very nature, they are faith-filled, infusing you with supernatural strength and enabling you to pray more effectively. Paul's prayers will challenge you to grow spiritually and see God's plans realized in the lives of those around you. His prayers are aimed at building spiritual vigor—the power Jesus called "virtue"—so that you might become a world-changer. They are spiritual exercises designed to produce spiritual muscle. It is only with this spiritual might that you can live the victorious and supernatural life to which He has called each of us.

For this reason, we are honored to present this book, *Discover the Power in the Prayers of Paul,* to provide you with an opportunity to take a deeper look at the prayers of Paul singularly and as a whole. To do this, we have organized this book into three parts:

PART ONE includes Paul's teaching on prayer, along with an exploration of the themes resident in each major prayer. Our goal is to learn more about what they teach us, what they are asking for, and how they fit into the body of Paul's writing. Various translations are included so you can better see the intricate balance of meaning as well as the context in which Paul presented each one.

PART TWO includes paraphrases of these scriptural prayers so that you can pray them for yourself, your loved ones, your government and church leaders, your church, community—anyone, in fact, for whom you feel led to pray.

PART THREE is an in-depth look at the life of Paul. This will shed light on why Paul was praying a specific prayer for a particular group of people or individuals.

Paul's prayers reveal overlooked keys to living the extraordinary life in the Spirit that Jesus died to give each of us. It is our hope that as you read, study, meditate upon, and pray these Spirit-inspired prayers, you will understand the depths of God's love for you, discover the grace and power available to you as His beloved child, and increasingly live in the fullness of Jesus' desires for you, your loved ones, and your world.

Part **1** *One*

PAUL'S TEACHING ON PRAYER

INTRODUCTION

Pray without ceasing.
1 Thessalonians 5:17

What Jesus did on the Cross changed everything. Because of the Cross the Holy Spirit could come to live in the hearts of believers—regular people just like you and me. Suddenly there were new rules about how we come to know God, how we hear from Him, and how we serve Him. And certainly the very definition of prayer was altered forever.

Jesus described it this way:

> "I tell you the truth. It is to your advantage that I go away; for if I do not go away, the Helper [Holy Spirit] will not come to you; but if I depart, I will send Him to you."
>
> —*John 16:7* NKJV

Jesus proclaimed a radical departure from a religious lifestyle— turning religion inside out. With the coming of the Holy Spirit to indwell believers and endue them with power, it was no longer necessary to try to apply outside laws to their hearts, but rather the life of the Spirit within overflows with goodness, changing the world around it. Jesus taught the world what this change would mean and accomplished the transition through His death, burial, and resurrection. Then God called Paul to teach others how to live this radical new way of life.

For many years, Paul's great, personal zeal for the Law led him to fight against the teachings of Jesus. Even later in life, a devout and fully committed Paul called himself the chief of all sinners, referencing his role as persecutor of Jesus' followers. It was by divine revelation that he came to understand the utter failure of the Law to bring righteousness. Now he stands as spokesperson for the new order of believers—those who would know Jesus completely through revelation of the heart. Paul demonstrated that believers can walk in intimate relationship with Jesus. Whereas His disciples walked and talked with Him physically, believers are now able to enter into a spiritual walk—minute-by-minute communication and collaboration with Him through the vehicle of prayer.

If you are willing, you, too, can walk in the world-changing power of God's presence as Paul did. You, too, can find that power through prayer that accesses the deepest, most intimate relationship with God.

"INSTANT" IN PRAYER

One of the first things Paul teaches us is that prayer is much more than a spiritual discipline to be entered into during certain times and seasons. It should instead be as close and as regular as your breath, integrated into every fiber of your being.

In the Old Testament, those who honored and obeyed God found their way to certain places to pray—places where the presence of God was said to dwell, places such as the Temple. However, at Jesus' death, the Bible says the veil in the temple that separated the common people from the Holy of Holies—literally the presence of God—was torn from top to bottom. God's presence on earth was no longer confined to one particular place. As Jesus had promised, the Holy Spirit would now dwell in the hearts of believers, those who choose to make Jesus their Lord and Savior.

Jesus gave His disciples the following instruction: "When you pray, go into your room, and when you have shut your door, pray to your Father who is in the secret place; and your Father who sees in secret will reward you openly" (Matthew 6:6 NKJV). But Paul captures the essence of the New Covenant in his enlightened words: "Pray without ceasing" (1 Thessalonians 5:17). No longer will believers need to find secret places to pray—as Jesus instructed. Instead, believers now have a constant connection. The place of prayer is now within the believer—within you—in every step as you walk out your purpose here on earth.

Jesus instructed His disciples not to be showy in empty prayers, trying to impress others with their religious prowess. Paul teaches that God is now living within, as close and as constant as your breath.

This doesn't mean that there aren't times you shouldn't pull away from this chaotic world to be alone and hear God more clearly. That is truly needed from time to time. However, even in the midst of the chaos and challenges of life, God wants you to know and realize that there is never a time when you are alone, and never a time when the Spirit of God is not immediately present to help you. As breathing is crucial to your life in the natural, so prayer is crucial to your spiritual life.

Paul teaches that God loves you so much that He wants you to talk to Him continually and invite Him into every area of your life—all your joys, sorrows, triumphs, challenges, aspirations, and concerns.

Perhaps this explains why Paul so frequently intermingled his prayers with his writing. They had become as close as his thoughts and flowed comfortably into his letters. It can truly be said of Paul that he "prayed without ceasing."

A NEW CONNECTION BETWEEN PRAYER AND PEACE

While prayer in the Old Testament was to influence God to move on behalf of those on earth, after the Cross, prayer functioned to bring what God had already done from Heaven to earth by faith. It is now through believing prayer that the kingdom of God on earth—righteousness and peace and joy in the Holy Ghost—expands (Romans 14:17). Prayer is your access to all the things of the Spirit—whether it be the fruit or the gifts—a conduit which should be kept open at all times. There is a time for short prayers that might be no more than a sentence long, and there are other times when prayer demands a perseverance and diligence likened to the travail of childbirth (Galatians 4:19). Yet for you, the steadfast believer, both are to end in God's peace and joy, just as Paul wrote to the Philippians from his prison cell:

> Be anxious for nothing, but in everything by prayer
> and supplication, with thanksgiving, let your requests
> be made known to God; and the peace of God, which
> surpasses all understanding, will guard your hearts and
> minds through Christ Jesus.
>
> —*Philippians 4:6-7* NKJV

Paul's "formula" for prayer is very clear. Have a concern? Pray. Right then, right there, and continue to pray until the peace of God floods your soul and you know you have the answer. Then thank God for answering even before you see the physical manifestation of what you've asked for.

Perhaps you have time for only a short prayer now—what Pastor Rick Warren calls a "breath prayer." The answer does not lie in the length of your prayer or in the amount of time you spend meditating on the problem. The answer for every worry, stress, and anxiety comes from laying it before God and listening to His Spirit for the answer. Pray now and follow up when you can focus on hearing what God has to say to you.

To Paul, this is your way of "continuing instant in prayer" (Romans 12:12). Any trouble is a call to pray instantly, any joy a call to praise and thanksgiving. And a prayer that brings in God's peace is an answered prayer, even if there is no way in the natural that having peace in this matter makes sense. That is why it is called "peace which surpasses all understanding."

Paul also relied upon the Holy Spirit to know when to pray for others. Repeatedly in his letters, Paul says things such as, "I thank my God upon every remembrance of you" (Philippians 1:3; see 2 Timothy 1:3), or, "I make mention of you in my prayers." (See Romans 1:9; Ephesians 1:16; 1 Thessalonians 1:2; Philemon 4.) Think for a moment about how many people and how many churches Paul had to pray for. Paul's habit must have been that as he thought of someone, he would instantly "make mention" of them to God. It may have been a short one-sentence prayer or perhaps more, but it seems certain that Paul didn't stop and pray an hour or so for each person every day.

And Scripture confirms that Paul did not pray for people only when they "needed" prayer. Throughout his letters we see Paul praying for the members of Christ's church each time he heard reports of their love and faith, good reports, reports that they were prospering. He didn't wait for prayer requests; instead, he prayed a short prayer, "making mention of them" whenever they came to mind. To think of them was his signal to pray for them. How greatly would such an approach to prayer for others revolutionize our churches and missions today? Would we pray more for them or less?

THE HOLY SPIRIT AND PRAYER

After the death and resurrection of Jesus Christ, the whole context of relationship with God changed. Obedient devotees no longer lived by the letter of God's Law. Instead they lived by the power of the Holy Spirit. They lived by the Law of Love. After the Day of Pentecost, the changes in relationship with God brought about changes in the way we communicate with Him. Prayer has become an "inside job." The Holy Spirit not only provides the motivation to pray but also the understanding of what and how to pray. As Paul said in his letter to the Romans:

> Likewise the Spirit also helps in our weaknesses. *For we do not know what we should pray for as we ought, but the Spirit Himself makes intercession for us* with groanings which cannot be uttered. Now He who searches the hearts knows what the mind of the Spirit is, because He makes intercession for the saints according to the will of God.
>
> —*Romans 8:26-27* NKJV (emphasis added)

As a Christian you are quite literally "Spirit-filled." The Holy Spirit dwelling within you helps you as you strive to pray according to God's will. Paul's example here is that as the earth groans to be free of sin and under the jurisdiction of its Creator again, so the Spirit of God makes intercession through you for God's kingdom to grow on the earth. If you will ask the Holy Spirit to guide you in prayer and will yourself be sensitive to His leading, you can then pray in accordance with His understanding rather than your own. And in so doing, God's vast resources and abilities are applied to your petition. What a promise God has given! He himself will even help you pray as you should.

While many prayers can be short and still powerful (such as Jesus' prayer when He raised Lazarus from the dead)—just two verses long—prayer in the Spirit often takes perseverance and determination. As Paul advised the Ephesians:

> My brethren, be strong in the Lord and in the power
> of His might. Put on the whole armor of God, that
> you may be able to stand against the wiles of the devil.
> For we do not wrestle against flesh and blood, but
> against principalities, against powers, against the rulers
> of the darkness of this age, against spiritual hosts of
> wickedness in the heavenly places.... Praying always
> with all prayer and supplication in the Spirit, *being
> watchful to this end with all perseverance and supplica-
> tion for all the saints.*
>
> —*Ephesians 6:10-12, 18* NKJV (emphasis added)

To what end should you be watchful and pray with all perseverance? To the end that you are not struggling against other human beings, but against the principalities and powers who influence them. While God's answer comes immediately, there is a time when persistent prayer is necessary to bring that answer to earth. There is a battle in the heaven-lies to be fought for you just as there was for Daniel:

> He said to me, "Do not fear, Daniel, for from the first
> day that you set your heart to understand, and to

humble yourself before your God, your words were heard; and I have come because of your words. But the prince of the kingdom of Persia withstood me twenty-one days; and behold, Michael, one of the chief princes, came to help me, for I had been left alone there with the kings of Persia.

—*Daniel 10:12-13* NKJV

However, for those of us in the church age, it is not an angel who comes to help us, but rather the Holy Spirit himself. How can you fail to take advantage of that kind of help? How can your prayers possibly be ineffective? As Romans 8:31 (NIV) says, "What, then, shall we say in response to this? If God is for us, who can be against us?"

The Holy Spirit will always lead you to pray according to God's will, but He has provided yet another tool to help you better understand His will as you pray—the Bible. The Bible was written by many different authors, but they had one thing in common. They wrote down the words given to them by the Holy Spirit—the very same Holy Spirit who indwells and inspires you.

The Bible serves as God's system of checks and balances, His way of being sure that your prayers are not tainted by the waywardness of your own human mind. When you pray God's promises back to Him, you can pray with confidence, knowing that you are praying according to His will.

THE ORDER OF PRAYER

While every concern or worry is an instant call to prayer, something that should allow you to live constantly in God's peace, Paul also teaches that you should pray for others regularly regardless of your own situation. In fact, Paul urged those to whom he wrote to continually pray for others, including himself, even as he continually prayed for them. He constantly calls for prayer for those sowing the Gospel, as if that sowing would be of little effect unless the ministry fields were first cleared and plowed through prayer. In this Paul indicated another principle of the New Covenant: prayer leads to fruitfulness. That's why Paul instructed believers to always begin prayer in the same way:

> I exhort therefore that, *first of all,* supplications, prayers, intercessions, and giving of thanks, be made for all men; for kings, and for all that are in authority; *that we may lead a quiet and peaceable life in all godliness and honesty....* I will therefore that men pray every where, lifting up holy hands, without wrath and doubting.
>
> —*1 Timothy 2:1-2, 8* (emphasis added)

Why should we pray for our leaders? "That we may lead a quiet and peaceable life in all godliness and honesty." Paul wrote these words from prison on the eve of the first major Roman persecution of Christians under Nero as he understood the hindrance leaders could be to the Gospel flowing in any area, and the power they had to obstruct even those living honest and godly lives.

While this may have been especially true when it was written, it is just as true today. We experience this on many levels every day. For instance, in a work environment, telling the truth may get you into more trouble than just going with the flow. And letting others know you are a Christian may make working with them more difficult. Laws governing the workplace may make it difficult to express your faith in Jesus.

In some other parts of the world, matters are even worse. In spite of the extreme persecution suffered by the early Christians, nearly two-thirds of all Christians martyred for their faith died in the twentieth century, not the first! In fact, according to current estimates, more than 435 believers lose their lives every day because of their faith in Jesus Christ.[1] You have more need to pray for your leaders and lawmakers today then ever before—and, not only for those in your own nation but also for those from other nations. In fact, the more you pray for the leaders of other nations, the easier it will be to live a godly and honest life.

PRAYER AND THANKSGIVING

Almost everywhere Paul mentions prayer in his letters, he also discusses thanksgiving, as if the two were inseparable. While prayer may start with supplications (prayers that lay before God "a wanting or a need"[2]), and then move on to intercessions ("prayer, petition, or entreaty in favor of another"[3]), for Paul, time in prayer always began and ended with praise and thanksgiving.

In fact, getting to that praise and thanksgiving seems to be the goal of almost everything Paul teaches on prayer. To lay a concern before the Lord is to settle it. Thus prayer always ends in thanking God for the answer. If you are still anxious about something as you pray, your prayer is not yet complete. You need to continue to pray about it until you can earnestly thank God for the answer, as Paul said, "Continue earnestly in prayer, being vigilant in it with thanksgiving" (Colossians 4:2 NKJV). You might even say he meant you to "be vigilant in prayer until you can give thanksgiving." A prayer that ends before thanking God for His answer is a prayer without faith. As it says in Hebrews:

> Without faith it is impossible to please Him, for he
> who comes to God must believe that He is, and that
> He is a rewarder of those who diligently seek Him.
>
> —*Hebrews 11:6* NKJV

If you believe God is, that He is a rewarder, and that He has heard
your prayer, how can you end prayer in any other way than by thanking God for the answer? As John said:

> This is the confidence that we have in Him, that if
> we ask anything according to His will, He hears us.
> And if we know that He hears us, whatever we ask,
> we know that we have the petitions that we have
> asked of Him.
>
> —*1 John 5:14-15* NKJV

For God to hear a prayer is for Him to answer it. Thus, praising God
for who He is always makes for a good beginning, and thanking Him
for His goodness, peace, and answer always closes the door on doubt
and unbelief.

PAUL'S HOLY SPIRIT-INSPIRED PRAYERS

Paul wrote his letters to the churches through the power of the
indwelling Holy Spirit. Therefore, his prayers in those letters are truly
the words of the Holy Spirit praying through him. For each thing the
Holy Spirit taught through Paul, He quickened a spiritual muscle
within the believer—a muscle that would be exercised and trained by
reading Paul's epistles. As each need was revealed, Paul was quick to
raise it back to the Father in prayer, and those prayers flowed out of

Paul's heart, through his pen, and into his letters to be preserved for us. Today they are just as fresh as they were to those who first received them. Just as God spoke to the new believers in Greece, Macedonia, Asia Minor, and Rome through these letters, He speaks with equal life-giving power and revelation to us today. More than any other books of the Bible, the Epistles are for those living in our time.

As you look at the following chapters, God will encourage you to read, meditate, and reflect upon the meanings of Paul's prayers and begin to pray God's Word back to Him. You can use these prayers as part of your daily quiet times. You, your loved ones, and your world desperately need God's anointing and power. These Holy Spirit-inspired prayers, prayed by you in faith, will prove to be powerful and effective in their working. They contain the power to change your life and the lives of countless others.

Get ready for the God of miracles to work in and through you as you pray the prayers of Paul. Expect a spiritual transformation. Expect to see your world turned inside out. Let God develop in you and through you the spiritual muscle He wants you to have for such a time as this.

chapter one

GRANT ME A SPIRIT OF
WISDOM AND REVELATION

I also, after I heard of your faith in the Lord Jesus, and love unto
all the saints, cease not to give thanks for you, making mention
of you in my prayers; that the God of our Lord Jesus Christ, the
Father of glory, may give unto you the spirit of wisdom and
revelation in the knowledge of him: the eyes of your
understanding being enlightened; that ye may know what is the
hope of his calling, and what the riches of the glory of his
inheritance in the saints, and what is the exceeding greatness of
his power to us-ward who believe, according to the working of
his mighty power, which he wrought in Christ, when he raised
him from the dead, and set him at his own right hand in the
heavenly places, far above all principality, and power, and might,
and dominion, and every name that is named, not only in this
world, but also in that which is to come: and hath put all things
under his feet, and gave him to be the head over all things to the
church, which is his body, the fulness of him that filleth all in all.
Ephesians 1:15-23

If you were going to write one final letter to your children, what
would you say? What would you write to those who had attended
church with you and shared in the vision of reaching your community

with the love of God? What would you pray for them, knowing you would not see them again until you meet in heaven?

No church saw more miracles or matured more quickly than the one in Ephesus. Other than Corinth and eventually Rome, there were no other cities where Paul spent more time in his missionary travels. It was while Paul was in Ephesus that handkerchiefs and aprons were sent to him so that he could lay his hands on them, pray, and then send them out with God's healing and delivering power still held in the fabric (Acts 19:12). It was in Ephesus that the seven sons of Sceva were so impressed by the power of the Gospel that they tried to cast out a demon in the name of "the Jesus whom Paul preaches" (v. 13 NKJV).

Of all the churches Paul planted, it was only the Ephesian elders he summoned to meet him on what he knew would be his last journey to Jerusalem before being sent to Rome as a prisoner. The book of Ephesians was one of the last books Paul wrote, and two of his last three letters were written to Timothy, whom he had left to oversee things there. This includes 2 Timothy in which Paul bid his final farewell, stating he had "fought the good fight,…finished the race, [and]…kept the faith" (2 Timothy 4:7 NKJV [insert added]. In other words, Paul had accomplished the mission God had given him on the earth.

In essence, Paul's letter to the Ephesians was just such a last letter to loved ones, and Paul's prayers for them are his longest and deepest. Paul wrote the Ephesians from his first Roman imprisonment with the thought he would never travel east again. Instead, if he had the chance, he would take the gospel west to Spain.

Paul's first prayer for the Ephesians encompasses almost the entire first chapter, beginning with Paul's praise and thanksgiving for all that God had given to believers through Jesus Christ:

> Blessed be the God and Father of our Lord Jesus
> Christ, *who has blessed us with every spiritual blessing in*
> *the heavenly places in Christ.*
>
> —*Ephesians 1:3* NKJV (emphasis added)

Some of the blessings Paul lists:

1. God, before the foundations of the earth, chose us in Christ to be holy and blameless before Him (v. 4).

2. God predestined that we would be adopted as sons and daughters (v. 5).

3. God has made known to us the mystery of His will (v. 9).

4. God has given us an inheritance so that we can be to the praise of His glory (v. 12).

5. God, after we believed the truth of the Gospel, sealed us with the Holy Spirit to mark us as His redeemed possession (vv. 13-14).

At this point in the prayer, Paul switches from praise and thanksgiving to supplication and intercession on behalf of the Ephesians praying: *For this reason, ever since I heard of your faith in the Lord Jesus and your love for all God's people, I have not stopped giving thanks to God for you. I remember you in my prayers, and ask the God of our Lord Jesus Christ, the glorious Father, to:*

(a) *Give you the Spirit, who will make you wise and reveal God to you, so that you will know him.*

(b) *Open your minds to see his light, so that you will know to what hope he has called you.*

(c) *Cause you to understand how rich are the wonderful blessings he promises his people.*

(d) Help you to understand how very great is his power at work in us who believe.

This power in us is the same as the mighty strength which he used when he raised Christ from death and seated him at his right side in the heavenly world. Christ rules there above all heavenly rulers, authorities, powers, and lords; he is above all titles of power in this world and in the next. God put all things under Christ's feet, and gave him to the church as supreme Lord over all things. The church is Christ's body, the completion of him who himself completes all things everywhere.

—(Ephesians 1:15-23 TEV*) (verses 18-23* PARAPHRASED*)*

These four requests summarize what all believers need to know in order to fulfill their mission on the earth—a prayer needed as much for believers today as it was in the first century.

KNOWING GOD

The greatest promise of Christianity is that we can know God.

Think about that for a minute—you and I, puny specks of dust on one of billions upon billions of planets revolving around billions upon billions of stars in a seemingly infinite universe, have been promised that we can intimately know the Creator of it all.

Take a look at these scriptural promises:

"I will put My law within them and on their heart I will write it; and I will be their God, and they shall be My people. They will not teach again, each man his neighbor and each man his brother, saying, 'Know the LORD,' *for they will all know Me, from the least of them to the greatest of them*," declares the LORD, "for I will forgive their iniquity, and their sin I will remember no more."

—*Jeremiah 31:33-34* NASB (emphasis added)

Draw near to God and He will draw near to you.

—*James 4:8* NASB

Beloved, let us love one another, for love is from God; and everyone who loves is born of God and *knows God.*

—*1 John 4:7* NASB (emphasis added)

On the night He was arrested, Jesus prayed for us. What was the first request in His prayer?

"This is eternal life, *that they may know You,* the only true God, and Jesus Christ whom You have sent."

—*John 17:3* NASB (emphasis added)

As James said, "You do not have because you do not ask. You ask and do not receive, because you ask amiss" (James 4:2-3 NKJV). If we feel that we do not know God, then it is either because we haven't ever asked to know Him or have never shown the steadfastness and faith to continue seeking Him until we truly begin the process of knowing Him. The very beginning of eternal life is the initial knowing of God, and that knowing of and learning more and more about God is the quest we will remain steadfast to for all eternity.

Notice though that Paul doesn't pray only that we would "know God," but that we would have "a spirit of wisdom and revelation" in knowing Him. Thus knowing God would be not only spiritual revelation through the Holy Spirit as Paul experienced in meeting Jesus, but it would also include wisdom. Many ministers teach that knowledge is what we can know in our minds as individual facts and truths; however, wisdom is the ability to successfully apply that knowledge to whatever we are doing. One is of the intellect, the other practical. One is found in the Word of God; the other through the leadership of the Holy Ghost—in essence, it is living by the balance of the Word and the Spirit. Thus Paul is praying that we intellectually know about God, that we spiritually get the revelation of Him, and that we have His wisdom to know what to do to increase His kingdom in our lives and throughout our world.

KNOWING THE HOPE OF HIS CALLING

First Corinthians 13:13 tells us hope is one of the three most lasting things in the universe. In Romans 8:24, Paul reveals that hope is necessary for salvation from a God we have not yet seen—in essence we must first have the hope that He exists before we can have the faith that He does. Without hope, we cannot have faith. As Paul says it, "we are saved by hope" (Romans 8:24). Many ministers in recent years have called hope "the blueprint for faith." In other words, hope plans, faith realizes.

Until you can hope for something, you have no chance of ever believing that you will one day see it. As it says in Hebrews:

> Faith *is the substance of things hoped for,* the evidence of things not seen.
> —*Hebrews 11:1* (emphasis added)

Hope creates the vision for what you want to accomplish; faith is the day-to-day walking out of that vision. But without first having that vision, faith has nothing to give substance to. Thus, your faith needs hope in order to work effectively.

According to the dictionary, hope means: "desire accompanied by expectation of or belief in fulfillment,"[4] or "favorable and confident expectation."[5] In other words, even the foundation for your seeking God—your desire to know God as He wants you to know Him—is based in hope. Only if you hope (have a confident expectation) that you can know Him will you ever begin to truly seek Him.

Paul is praying here for our dreams and aspirations to become vivid and tangible. He is praying we will receive the "hope of our calling"—a vision of why God called us before the foundations of the earth.

In other words, he is praying that you will be able to clearly see why—out of all the six billion plus people on planet earth—He called you specifically to accomplish the unique purpose for which He made you, and that you would begin to earnestly expect that purpose to be fulfilled as you follow the leading of His Holy Spirit.

No one starts a journey they have no hope of finishing, but many with hope will finish journeys they had never imagined they would begin. Whatever answer you are looking for from God begins with your hope of receiving that answer. Why not take the time right now to ask God to give you His supernatural hope and fill you with the confident expectation that what He started in you He will complete? Ask Him, by the power of the Holy Spirit, to revive in you and your loved ones the dreams and desires He placed there and to rekindle the passion for Him and His kingdom that was once burning brightly. The adversary of your soul is determined to steal and extinguish your hope so that you cannot fight the good fight of faith and fulfill God's purposes for your life. But the "God of all hope" wants to fill you with His joy and peace in believing, so that you will abound in hope and walk in victory. It is time to start praying and believing that hope is yours for the asking—because it is. Don't give up on your dreams, and don't let go of the hope of your calling!

UNDERSTANDING THE RICHES OF OUR INHERITANCE

In Ephesians 1:11 and 12, Paul praises and thanks God for the inheritance we, as believers, have been given through Christ:

> In Him also we have obtained an inheritance, being predestined according to the purpose of Him who works all things according to the counsel of His will, that we who first trusted in Christ should be to the praise of His glory.
>
> —*Ephesians 1:11-12* NKJV

Then Paul turns around and prays that we would understand that inheritance:

> The eyes of your understanding being enlightened; that you may know ... what are the riches of the glory of His inheritance in the saints.
>
> —*Ephesians 1:18* NKJV

What does it really mean to be a child of God?

> The Spirit Himself bears witness with our spirit that
> we are children of God, and *if children, then heirs—*
> *heirs of God and joint heirs with Christ,* if indeed we
> suffer with Him, that we may also be glorified together.
>
> —*Romans 8:16-17* NKJV (emphasis added)

Paul calls us "joint heirs with Christ," meaning that all He inherited from His Father is also available to us—in fact, it is now ours in Him even as Jesus has already inherited it as He sits at the right hand of the Father.

If we already have this inheritance, then why aren't we experiencing the benefits of it? Paul explains it this way:

> The heir, as long as he is a child, differeth nothing from
> a servant, though he be lord of all; but is under tutors
> and governors until the time appointed of the father.
>
> —*Galatians 4:1-2*

In other words, until we grow up and realize all we have in Christ, that inheritance will be locked away in safekeeping until we do grow responsible enough to handle it.

Who is the tutor and governor who will take us into that inheritance? As Paul said earlier in Ephesians 1:

> Having believed, *you were sealed with the Holy Spirit of*
> *promise, who is the guarantee of our inheritance* until
> the redemption of the purchased possession, to the
> praise of His glory.
>
> —*Ephesians 1:13-14* NKJV (emphasis added)

The *King James Version* calls the indwelling of the Holy Spirit the "earnest of our inheritance." Just as a family would put down an earnest-money deposit on a house in order to show the sincerity of their offer to purchase it, so God puts the Holy Spirit into our hearts as a guarantee of our redemption. The Holy Spirit is also there to teach and guide us into all that this inheritance is for us—He is our tutor and guardian—just as Jesus promised:

> "When He, the Spirit of truth [the Holy Spirit], has come, He will guide you into all truth; for He will not speak on His own authority, but whatever He hears He will speak; and He will tell you things to come. He will glorify Me, for He will take of what is Mine and declare it to you. All things that the Father has are Mine. Therefore I said that *He will take of Mine and declare it to you.*"
>
> —*John 16:13-15* NKJV [insert and emphasis added]

How do we know when we have grown spiritually mature enough to collect some of that inheritance? Take a look at the order of Paul's prayer. First he prays for growth in *knowing God,* then for growth in *knowing and realizing our calling.* Then he prays that we would be able to understand our inheritance. So the purpose of our inheritance is clear. It is given to help us *fulfill our calling—or purpose—on the earth.* God made all His vast resources available to Jesus so He could fulfill His mission on the earth, and Jesus has made them available to us for the same purpose: that we might work wholeheartedly, just as Jesus did, to expand the kingdom of God on the earth during our lives here.

And to this very purpose, there was one other thing Paul felt that we needed—not only to understand the riches of our inheritance but also the power behind that inheritance.

UNDERSTANDING THE SURPASSING GREATNESS OF HIS POWER TOWARD US

Paul's final request is that we would understand "what is the exceeding greatness of His power toward us who believe" (Ephesians 1:19 NKJV). He spends the last part of this prayer describing that "surpassing greatness"

> These are in accordance with the working of the strength of His might which He brought about in Christ, when He raised Him from the dead and seated Him at His right hand in the heavenly places, far above all rule and authority and power and dominion, and every name that is named, not only in this age but also in the one to come. And He put all things in subjection under His feet, and gave Him as head over all things to the church, which is His body, the fullness of Him who fills all in all.
>
> —*Ephesians 1:19-23* NASB

Just as God raised Joseph from the depths of prison to the second highest position in the land of Egypt, so He raised Jesus from the depths of death—a sacrificial death for our sins—to the highest seat of authority in the entire universe at the right hand of Almighty God. With that act, Jesus also took the keys of hell and death from the devil so that God could now redeem us from the power of sin and adopt us again as His children. Think about that for a moment. Truly, there has been no greater act of power that has ever taken place in the history of time. And Paul is praying that all his requests here are made in accordance with the working of that strength.

Consider this for a moment: If God is making this power available to you to fulfill your purpose and mission on the earth, what power in the universe can stop you from being all God has called you to be?

PUTTING IT ALL TOGETHER

The devil's strategy to stop you is simple and obvious. If he can get you to focus on the setbacks you face or your own advancement and individual comfort on the earth—and the little and secondary things of life—he can defeat you. If you focus on the small, he can get you to overlook the great. You will then major in the minor things of life—the selfish things—and accomplish nothing. You will strain at gnats and swallow camels—and in so doing, completely miss God's purpose for your life.

But Paul is praying for you to realize just the opposite. First of all, you must understand how great and loving your Heavenly Father truly is. Second, you must receive hope—a vision—of the great things He has called you to do. Third, you must understand the amazing resources He has made available to you in order to accomplish that calling. And last of all, you must understand the miraculous power that is backing all of these up.

Are you facing physical illness? God raised Jesus from the dead to sit at His right hand in heaven. What illness can stand in light of that?

Are you facing a financial crisis? God raised Jesus from the dead to sit at His right hand in heaven. What financial crisis can stand in light of that?

Are you facing a problem in your family? God raised Jesus from the dead to sit at His right hand in heaven. What family problem can stand in light of that?

You fill in the blank. Now ask yourself what problem can stand in light of the fact that God raised Jesus from the dead to sit at His right hand in heaven?

Paul is praying that you will look at the big picture and see the hope you have in Christ rather than the hopelessness of your present situation. Faith can stretch its legs only when you have enough hope to lift up your head and look into the eyes of the One who has the power to help you. In this prayer, Paul is praying that you will receive a vision for your life, realizing your God-given purpose, and looking to God's greatness and the leadership of the Holy Spirit for its fulfillment.

It may take an instant or months or years to walk out whatever it is blocking your way at the moment, but it all starts with a prayer such as this one. Meditate on these scriptures and pray with Paul that your eyes will be opened to all God is and all that He has for you. That is your first step into His greater things.

PRAYING EPHESIANS 1:15-23 FOR YOURSELF

Father,

In the name of Jesus, I praise and thank You for all of the spiritual gifts You have bestowed upon me in Christ Jesus. I thank You that You have adopted me as Your child, that You have forgiven my sins, that You have promised to let me know the purposes for which You saved me, and the greatness of the inheritance You have prepared for me to accomplish that purpose. I also praise and thank You for sealing me with Your Holy Spirit to live within me and guide me—that Your fullness will be realized in my life as I follow and learn from Him day by day.

Because of these great blessings, Father, I pray that You will give me a spirit of revelation and knowledge in knowing You. Open the eyes of my understanding so that I will know the hope of Your calling. Help me to understand the riches of the glory of Your great inheritance to me through Jesus Christ because I have believed on and trusted in You. Cause me to come to understand the exceedingly great power You have made available to me to accomplish what You have called me to do.

Father, I thank You that all these things are accomplished according to Your exceedingly great strength—the very power by which You sent Your Son, Jesus, to earth to die on the Cross for my sins, and by which You raised Him from the dead to sit at Your right hand in the heavens, far above any other ruler, authority, power, or kingdom; above every name that is named, not only in this world, but in the world to come; with all things under His feet; and as the head of all parts of the universal Church, which is His Body on the earth, left here to accomplish His goals and purposes as His fullness to all humankind.

Amen.

PRAYING EPHESIANS 1:15-23 FOR OTHERS

Father,

In the name of Jesus, I praise and thank You for all of the spiritual gifts You have bestowed upon _____ in Christ Jesus. I thank

*You that You have adopted _____ as Your own child, and that
You have forgiven all of _____ sins. I thank You for all of Your
promises that You will reveal to _____, Your divine purpose and
calling for _____ life, and that _____ would understand the
greatness of the inheritance You have prepared for _____ to
accomplish that purpose and calling. I also praise and thank You
for sealing _____ with Your Holy Spirit to live within _____
and guide _____ into all of Your fullness.*

*Because of these great blessings, Father, I pray that You will give
_____ a spirit of revelation and knowledge in knowing You.
Open _____'s eyes of understanding so that _____ would know
the full hope of Your calling. Help _____ to understand the riches
of the glory of Your great inheritance for _____ through Jesus
Christ because _____ has believed on and trusted in You. Cause
_____ to come to understand the exceedingly great power You
have made available to _____ to accomplish what You have
called _____ to do on this earth.*

*Father: I thank You that all of these requests will be accomplished
according to Your exceedingly great power—the very power by
which You sent Your Son, Jesus, to the earth to die on the Cross for
our sins, and by which You raised Him from the dead to sit at
Your right hand in the heavens, far above any other ruler, authority, power, or kingdom; above every name that is named, not only
in this world, but in the world to come; with all things under His
feet; and as the head of all parts of the universal Church, which is
His Body on the earth, left here to accomplish His goals and
purposes as His fullness to all humankind.*

Amen.

PAUL'S PRAYER IN CONTEXT THROUGH VARIOUS TRANSLATIONS

Ephesians 1:3-23 from the *New American Standard Bible*® (NASB)

Blessed be the God and Father of our Lord Jesus Christ, who has blessed us with every spiritual blessing in the heavenly places in Christ, just as He chose us in Him before the foundation of the world, that we would be holy and blameless before Him.

In love He predestined us to adoption as sons through Jesus Christ to Himself, according to the kind intention of His will, to the praise of the glory of His grace, which He freely bestowed on us in the Beloved.

In Him we have redemption through His blood, the forgiveness of our trespasses, according to the riches of His grace which He lavished on us.

In all wisdom and insight He made known to us the mystery of His will, according to His kind intention which He purposed in Him with a view to an administration suitable to the fullness of the times, that is, the summing up of all things in Christ, things in the heavens and things on the earth.

In Him also we have obtained an inheritance, having been predestined according to His purpose who works all things after the counsel of His will, to the end that we who were the first to hope in Christ would be to the praise of His glory.

In Him, you also, after listening to the message of truth, the gospel of your salvation—having also believed, you were sealed in Him with the Holy Spirit of promise, who is given as a pledge of our inheritance, with a view to the redemption of God's own possession, to the praise of His glory.

For this reason I too, having heard of the faith in the Lord Jesus which exists among you and your love for all the saints, do not cease giving thanks for you, while making mention of you in my prayers; that the God of our Lord Jesus Christ, the Father of glory, may give to you a spirit of wisdom and of revelation in the knowledge of Him.

I pray that the eyes of your heart may be enlightened, so that you will know what is the hope of His calling, what are the riches of the glory of His inheritance in the saints, and what is the surpassing greatness of His power toward us who believe.

These are in accordance with the working of the strength of His might which He brought about in Christ, when He raised Him from the dead and seated Him at His right hand in the heavenly places, far above all rule and authority and power and dominion, and every name that is named, not only in this age but also in the one to come.

And He put all things in subjection under His feet, and gave Him as head over all things to the church, which is His body, the fullness of Him who fills all in all.

Ephesians 1:3-23 from *The Message*® (THE MESSAGE)

How blessed is God! And what a blessing he is! He's the Father of our Master, Jesus Christ, and takes us to the high places of blessing in him. Long before he laid down earth's foundations, he had us in mind, had settled on us as the focus of his love, to be made whole and holy by his love. Long, long ago he decided to adopt us into his family through Jesus Christ. (What pleasure he took in planning this!) He wanted us to enter into the celebration of his lavish gift-giving by the hand of his beloved Son.

Because of the sacrifice of the Messiah, his blood poured out on the altar of the Cross, we're a free people—free of penalties and punishments chalked up by all our misdeeds. And not just barely free, either. Abundantly free! He thought of everything, provided for everything we could possibly need, letting us in on the plans he took such delight in making. He set it all out before us in Christ, a long-range plan in which everything would be brought together and summed up in him, everything in deepest heaven, everything on planet earth.

It's in Christ that we find out who we are and what we are living for. Long before we first heard of Christ and got our hopes up, he had his eye on us, had designs on us for glorious living, part of the overall purpose he is working out in everything and everyone.

It's in Christ that you, once you heard the truth and believed it (this Message of your salvation), found yourselves home free— signed, sealed, and delivered by the Holy Spirit. This signet from God is the first installment on what's coming, a reminder that we'll get everything God has planned for us, a praising and glorious life.

That's why, when I heard of the solid trust you have in the Master Jesus and your outpouring of love to all the Christians, I couldn't stop thanking God for you—every time I prayed, I'd think of you and give thanks. But I do more than thank. I ask— ask the God of our Master, Jesus Christ, the God of glory—to

make you intelligent and discerning in knowing him personally,
your eyes focused and clear, so that you can see exactly what it is
he is calling you to do, grasp the immensity of this glorious way
of life he has for Christians, oh, the utter extravagance of his
work in us who trust him—endless energy, boundless strength!

All this energy issues from Christ: God raised him from death
and set him on a throne in deep heaven, in charge of running
the universe, everything from galaxies to governments, no
name and no power exempt from his rule. And not just for the
time being, but forever. He is in charge of it all, has the final
word on everything. At the center of all this, Christ rules the
church. The church, you see, is not peripheral to the world;
the world is peripheral to the church. The church is Christ's
Body, in which he speaks and acts, by which he fills everything
with his presence.

Ephesians 1:3-23 from the *International Standard Version®* (ISV)

Blessed be the God and Father of our Lord Jesus Christ! He
has blessed us in Christ with every spiritual blessing in the
heavenly realm, just as he chose us in him before the foundation of the world to be holy and blameless in his presence. In
love he predestined us for adoption to himself through Jesus
Christ, according to the pleasure of his will, so that we would
praise his glorious grace that he gave us in the Beloved One. In
him we have redemption through his blood, the forgiveness of
our offenses, according to the riches of God's grace that he
lavished on us, along with all wisdom and understanding,
when he made known to us the secret of his will. This was
according to his plan that he set forth in Christ to usher in the

fullness of the times and to gather up all things in Christ, both things in heaven and things on earth.

In Christ we were also chosen when we were predestined according to the purpose of the one who does everything according to the intention of his will, so that we who had already fixed our hope on Christ might live for his praise and glory. You, too, have heard the word of truth, the gospel of your salvation. When you believed in him you were sealed with the promised Holy Spirit, who is the guarantee of our inheritance until the redemption of God's own possession, to his praise and glory.

Therefore, because I have heard about your faith in the Lord Jesus and your love for all the saints, I never stop giving thanks for you as I mention you in my prayers. I pray that the God of our Lord Jesus Christ, the Father most glorious, would give you a spirit of wisdom and revelation through knowing Christ fully. Then, with the eyes of your hearts enlightened, you will know the hope of his calling, the riches of his glorious inheritance among the saints, and the unlimited greatness of his power for us who believe, according to the working of his mighty strength, which he put to work in Christ when he raised him from the dead and seated him at his right hand in the heavenly realm. He is far above every ruler, authority, power, dominion, and every name that can be named, not only in the present age but also in the one to come. God has put everything under his feet and has made him the head of everything for the good of the church, which is his body, the fullness of the one who fills everything in every way.

chapter two

STRENGTHEN ME TO LIVE BY YOUR LOVE

For this cause I bow my knees unto the Father of our Lord Jesus
Christ, of whom the whole family in heaven and earth is
named, that he would grant you, according to the riches of his
glory, to be strengthened with might by his Spirit in the inner
man; that Christ may dwell in your hearts by faith; that ye,
being rooted and grounded in love, may be able to comprehend
with all saints what is the breadth, and length, and depth,
and height; and to know the love of Christ, which passeth
knowledge, that ye might be filled with all the fulness of God.
Now unto him that is able to do exceeding abundantly above
all that we ask or think, according to the power that worketh
in us, unto him be glory in the church by Christ Jesus
throughout all ages, world without end. Amen.
Ephesians 3:14-21

It is one thing to know your purpose on the earth and the resources
available to fulfill it, but quite another to acquire those resources and
have the strength to walk out that purpose. Knowledge is one thing;
ability is another.

Our nation today is full of armchair quarterbacks—those who feel
they could better run the country or the church. Too many are
willing to give their opinions; too few are willing to work at making
things better.

While in Ephesians, chapter one, Paul prayed that you would receive a revelation of God, His purpose for your life, a glimpse of God's great inheritance for you, and an understanding of the power He has made available to you through Christ; in chapter three he prayed that you would develop the spiritual strength to make that knowledge effective and beneficial.

What inspired this prayer? In Ephesians, chapter two, and the first part of chapter three, Paul was speaking of the mystery of salvation that was to be revealed through the Church, while in the last verse of chapter one he called "[Christ's] body, the fullness of Him who fills all in all" (Ephesians 1:23 NKJV [insert added]). Paul then went on to state God's purpose from the beginning of time that He hoped to accomplish through Jesus:

> His intent was that now, through the church, the manifold wisdom of God should be made known to the rulers and authorities in the heavenly realms, according to his eternal purpose which he accomplished in Christ Jesus our Lord. In him and through faith in him we may approach God with freedom and confidence.
>
> —*Ephesians 3:10-12* NIV

God's intent and purpose was not that Christ would reveal God's plan and demonstrate His authority, but that the Church would! His plan was that the manifold wisdom of God would be so evident in the Church that all the principalities and powers in the heavenly realm would see it and understand the magnificence of God.

Once he had written this, Paul launched forth into prayer again: *For this reason, then, I fall on my knees before the Father, from whom every family in heaven and on earth receives its true name. I ask God, from the wealth of his glory, to:*

    (a) Strengthen you from the inside out by His Holy Spirit.

    (b) Allow Jesus to dwell—feel comfortably at home—in your hearts by faith.

    (c) Cause you to become rooted and grounded in the love of Jesus to the point of understanding and knowing its breadth, length, depth, and height with all the saints, even though that understanding is beyond any of us.

    (d) Fill you with all that God is—His power, His righteousness, His glory, His all!

I praise, thank, and give glory to God the Father who can do through us more than we have ever thought or hoped to accomplish on our own because we can operate according to His power working in us, not our own. May He be richly glorified in all that Jesus Christ accomplishes through His Body—the Church—throughout all the ages of this earth and beyond. Amen.

—*(Ephesians 3:14-21* GNT, PARAPHRASED*)*

Within this prayer, Paul is encouraging us to plug into the remarkable reservoir of stamina and ability available to every believer through Christ Jesus.

LIVING LIFE INSIDE OUT

It is also in this prayer that Paul deals with one of the most difficult transitions we face as believers—to change our focus from the natural world and live solely according to what we see, touch, taste, hear, smell, and learn from the physical world, to seeing, tasting, touching, hearing, learning, and drawing strength from the spiritual world. While in the natural, we exercise our minds and bodies to master the skills of living in the physical world. When we are born again, we must add the ability to renew our minds and exercise our human spirits to grow in the things of the spiritual realm. The nine fruit that grow in our human spirits and the nine gifts that come from the Holy Spirit, for example, are given by the Spirit to empower us to change things in our physical world—our families, our jobs, our churches, our communities, and our planet. In others words, it is not just physical exercise and experience that increase our ability but also spiritual exercise and experience—and our greater strength comes from the inside rather than the outside.

Throughout the New Testament we see references to our threefold nature—each of us is at the innermost part a spirit with a soul that lives in a body. The easiest of these three to recognize would be the physical body, the part we see with our natural eyes when we meet and talk with others or look at our own reflection. This flesh and blood body has five senses, along with countless instincts, reflexes, and feelings (hot, hungry, tired, etc.). But it isn't difficult to acknowledge that we are much more than merely bodies. Just under the thin surface, we have a soul—some might call it a personality—which consists of the mind, the will, and the emotions. The third part Paul prays specifically for here is the human spirit—the part that separates us from all other created beings. Paul calls this the "inner man" (Ephesians 3:16).

Some would say that the soul and spirit are one and the same. But before you decide, take a look at this scripture from God's Word:

> The word of God is living and powerful, and sharper
> than any two-edged sword, piercing even to *the divi-*
> *sion of soul and spirit,* and of joints and marrow, and is
> *a discerner of the thoughts and intents of the heart.*
>
> —*Hebrews 4:12* NKJV (emphasis added)

In other scriptures, we see Paul differentiate blessings for each of the three parts:

> May the God of peace Himself sanctify you completely;
> and *may your whole spirit, soul, and body* be preserved
> blameless at the coming of our Lord Jesus Christ.
>
> —*1 Thessalonians 5:23* NKJV (emphasis added)

Even Jesus refers to these three parts in the Great Commandment:

> "You shall love the LORD your God with all your heart
> [spirit], with all your soul, with all your mind [soul,
> again—the intellectual part], and with all your
> strength [body]."
>
> —*Mark 12:30* NKJV [inserts added]

Perhaps the easiest way to understand this is to imagine that your spirit is a mirror reflection of your body—and in the same way that your body interacts with the physical world, your spirit has the ability to interact with the spiritual world. Between the two is your soul, which takes input from all its sources—what the body experiences, what the mind reasons, what the emotions tell it, and what the spirit senses—in order to feed them into the will, which determines how you will respond. Every decision you make in life is made by interpreting this input, weighing and balancing it, and then drawing a conclusion.

Imagine for a moment that you are at a conference, where you had to walk a good distance to get to the main building. It is lunchtime and your body tells you it's hungry. You go to the concessions area, but you realize that your spouse left the money in the car. Your mind coldly and rationally gives you some options: you can go hungry, you can angrily insist that your spouse walk back to the car and get it, you can try to steal a sandwich while no one is looking, or you can walk back to the car yourself.

Your body insists that you need a food fix, so you eliminate the first option and move on. Your emotions tell you that you are angry—with your spouse, who carelessly left the lunch money in the car. But before you make the decision to retaliate, you remember the words of the conference speaker who encouraged you to be more forgiving and loving to your spouse. That input persuades you to eliminate option 2. That leaves swiping a sandwich, but your conscience quickly reminds you that it's wrong to steal. Finally, you see that this unfortunate situation has provided you with a great way to exercise love for your spouse, while satisfying your physical hunger and protecting your conscience— so you head back to the car to get your lunch money.

However, what happens if the fruit of love inside you is shriveled and barely alive? Well, you are likely to choose one of the other options. This scenario provides a picture of how the whole person comes together to make choices. Where one part is stronger or weaker than others, choices sometimes go awry.

You may be a person who is mostly controlled by your emotions, physical desire, a sense of cold, calculating reason, or you could be a person who subjugates these things in order to follow the direction of the Spirit of God within you—which is the goal of Paul's first request in this prayer.

If you are stronger on the inside than the out—filled with flourishing quantities of spiritual fruit: "love, joy, peace, patience, kindness, goodness, faithfulness, gentleness, and self-control" (Galatians 5:22-23 NIV)—and have your mind renewed to the spiritual wisdom of the Word of God so that you can discern what is coming from your spirit as opposed to your emotions and physical desires, then you will not only know what is the right thing to do, but you will have the inner strength to do it.

Yet Paul's prayer goes even further. He is also praying that you will not be ruled or limited by what is possible in the physical realm, but that you will develop the spiritual muscle to pull from the spiritual—through the gifts of the Spirit as the Holy Spirit directs—to change the physical world around you. As Jesus said, you are to pray that His will be done on earth as it is in heaven. When you develop spiritual might, you can become God's instruments for bringing His will to your world as He directs you. You then can become conduits through which spiritual blessings can flow into the natural world. Thus praying this prayer and meditating on the Word of God become spiritual exercises that increase your spiritual ability in the same way physical exercise, practicing of skills, and study can make you more effective in reaching your goals in the natural.

CHRIST ON THE INSIDE

Paul then prays "that Christ may dwell in your hearts by faith." Most of us learn that Jesus comes to live in our hearts when we are born again. Yet is this what Paul is talking about here? Or does this phrase have a different meaning in this instance?

Here, Paul is praying for what many ministers would call "Jesus-inside-mindedness"—in others words, that as we walk through each part of each day, we are faithfully conscious that Jesus is inside of us, flooding out evil or selfish desires and wrong thinking with His presence. It is living "What Would Jesus Do?" out of our hearts rather than our intellects. It is letting Jesus be "Jesus within us" to change the way we see things—the way we see what is possible and what is not—and create a spiritual reservoir of possibilities within us.

While Jesus walked the earth, His teachings and ministry seemed to focus on a few key points, all of them having to do with the way we see things. One seems to resonate with the Sermon on the Mount: "You have heard it said…but I say until you.…" No longer was it just what we say or see or do but also what we think or desire or fantasize about. He wanted us to change our focus from building a kingdom for ourselves on earth to building the kingdom of heaven. He wanted us to stretch our expectations from what *we* can do to what *God* can do.

Living "Jesus-inside-minded" puts a completely different spin on things—it is living on the earth through the eyes of heaven. Paul was praying that this "Jesus-inside-mindedness" would grow in each of us, because:

> There is therefore now no condemnation to those who are in Christ Jesus, who do not walk according to the flesh, but according to the Spirit. For the law of the Spirit of life in Christ Jesus has made me free from the law of sin and death. … For those who live according to the flesh set their minds on the things of the flesh,

but those who live according to the Spirit, the things
of the Spirit. For to be carnally minded is death, but
to be spiritually minded is life and peace.

—*Romans 8:1-2, 5-6* NKJV

Paul is praying that we dispose of the old and put on the new:

In reference to your former manner of life, you lay
aside the old self, which is being corrupted in accordance with the lusts of deceit, and that you be
renewed in the spirit of your mind, and put on the
new self, which in the likeness of God has been
created in righteousness and holiness of the truth.

—*Ephesians 4:22-24* NASB

Who is this "new self"? This new man is Christ. It is time that we let
Him fully live within and through us. But again, that is not all Paul is
praying for us in this prayer.

ROOTED DEEPLY AND FOUNDED SECURELY

It is interesting to note that Paul's supplications in Ephesians 3
mirror the ministry of the Godhead:

- Paul prays that the Holy Spirit would strengthen our human
  spirits with His might.

- Paul prays that Christ would live within us by faith.

- Paul prays that we would be filled with the fullness of God
  the Father.

Each of these requests is made simply and concisely. But then, right in the middle of this prayer, Paul cries out for an even deeper understanding—a reservoir of possibility and knowledge of the fullness of God:

> I bow my knees to the Father of our Lord Jesus
> Christ,…that you, being rooted and grounded in love,
> may be able to comprehend with all the saints what is
> the width and length and depth and height—to know
> the love of Christ which passes knowledge.
>
> —*Ephesians 3:14,17-19* NKJV

Paul is literally asking for us to gain a knowledge of the love of God beyond knowing. How do we get to know something that is beyond knowing?

One key lies again in the request that we comprehend this love "with all the saints." In other words, this knowledge of God's love is so great that it cannot be contained by one person—it is something that can be known only within the unity of a group of believers. In fact, it is a love that has an extra dimension. Objects in our world have three dimensions, but there are four dimensions to this love Paul is searching for words to describe—a corporate dimension. Paul wants the Ephesians to see that as the Body of Christ they can know Christ in a way that is not possible for the individual person.

Paul is also praying that the Ephesian Christians will be rooted and grounded in this love. What does this suggest? One thing is that they would be immovable and inseparable from it. To be rooted in something is to be so intertwined in it that we can never fully pull ourselves free. To be grounded in it is to have it as a base in a similar way to a house being built on a foundation. There is no firmer foundation than the love of Christ.

Trees and plants pull up through their roots the water and nutrients they need to live. If we are rooted in Christ's love, then our spirits will be watered and nourished. Thus this love acts again both to stabilize and strengthen us while at the same time overflowing from us to others. If we as the Church are to truly be the means of showing the universe the manifold wisdom of God, then it will be not only what is in us that will do it, but more importantly what flows from us. Paul's prayer is that it would be God's love that flows from us in all circumstances.

FILLED WITH THE FATHER'S FULLNESS

Paul is also praying here that we would be so filled with God that we are indistinguishable from His purposes on the earth, just as Jesus was:

> Jesus said to him, "Have I been with you so long, and yet you have not known Me, Philip? He who has seen Me has seen the Father; so how can you say, 'Show us the Father'? Do you not believe that I am in the Father, and the Father in Me? The words that I speak to you I do not speak on My own authority; but the Father who dwells in Me does the works. Believe Me that I am in the Father and the Father in Me, or else believe Me for the sake of the works themselves.

> "Most assuredly, I say to you, he who believes in Me, the works that I do he will do also; and greater works than these he will do, because I go to My Father."

> —*John 14:9-12* NKJV

Of the three persons of the Godhead—the Father, the Son, and the Holy Ghost—it seems that the Father is always the master planner, the Son is the implementer of that plan, and the Holy Spirit is the fulfiller and the glorifier of the plan. To have all three working together in us is to walk in the fullness of Christ as Paul described in Colossians:

> As you have received Christ Jesus the Lord, so walk in Him, having been firmly rooted and now being built up in Him and established in your faith, just as you were instructed, and overflowing with gratitude. See to it that no one takes you captive through philosophy and empty deception, according to the tradition of men, according to the elementary principles of the world, rather than according to Christ. *For in Him all the fullness of Deity dwells in bodily form,* and in Him you have been made complete, and He is the head over all rule and authority.
>
> —*Colossians 2:6-10* NASB (emphasis added)

And again in 2 Corinthians:

> The grace of the Lord Jesus Christ, and the love of God, and the communion of the Holy Ghost, be with you all. Amen.
>
> —*2 Corinthians 13:14*

In this benediction, Paul prays that the fullness of the Godhead would be with us through each of their main attributes:

1. The grace of Jesus exemplified as He walked the earth and taught and healed and was moved by compassion, not merit.

2. The love of the Father who created us that He might love us, sending Jesus to save us because of that love.

3. The communion or companionship and partnership of the Holy Spirit who is the one left with us to instruct and guide us into all God has for us.

This includes the fullness of the mission and plan of God being within us (as Paul prayed for in the Ephesians 1 prayer), as well as the fullness, fitness, and power to walk that mission and plan out on the earth (as he prayed for us in this prayer in Ephesians 3). It was through this fullness of God on the inside of us, through our human spirits and the fullness of God and His love pouring forth through our lives, that God would manifest His will to the universe and it would be far beyond what anyone had ever hoped.

BEYOND WHAT YOU'VE EVER ASKED OR IMAGINED

It has often been said that if you can't hope for something—if you can't get a vision of it or see it in your mind's eye—then you can never achieve it. Perhaps this is true for those who walk according to natural abilities, resources, and skills, but it is also true for those who know God and are willing to focus their eyes upon Him. He, "(in consequence of) the [action of His] power that is at work within us, is able to [carry out His purpose and] do superabundantly, far over and above all that we [dare] ask or think [infinitely beyond our highest prayers, desires, thoughts, hopes, or dreams]" (Ephesians 3:20 AMP [insert added]). In other words, if we can dream it, we can achieve it; but if we are to accomplish greater things than what we can envision, then we had better let God do the dreaming and let Him make His dreams real through us.

This is why Paul closes this prayer with praise and thanksgiving to the God who "is able to accomplish infinitely more than we would ever dare to ask or hope" (Ephesians 3:20 NLT), and then goes on to pray:

> To Him be the glory *in the church and in Christ Jesus*
> to all generations forever and ever. Amen.
>
> —*Ephesians 3:21* NASB (emphasis added)

In other words, Paul is praying that not only will God show His manifest wisdom through the Church, but He would also be glorified by the Church and all that it does, as well as through Christ Jesus His Son as Jesus leads and guides His Body on the earth.

GREATER THINGS

When Jesus was talking to the disciples the night He was arrested, he told them that if they would believe on Him, then they would do the things that He did as well as greater works than He did. Paul was likely among the first to really prove this promise true by spreading the Gospel throughout much of the known world and seeing it confirmed time and again with signs and wonders. Paul's desire was that, as he was finishing his race, those in the church in Ephesus would realize their own individual races, take the baton, and continue the spread of the Gospel around the world.

Paul had made an interesting discovery: the only life really worth living was one determined to see the kingdom of God expand and grow wherever the Gospel was sown. Paul's prayers here were that the heart of God would grab the readers and hearers of this epistle so intensely that they would plug into that life and be filled with anticipation as they waited to see God's kingdom manifested around them wherever they went. Paul was praying they would live in the fullness of the Spirit he had experienced.

By praying and meditating upon these Holy Spirit-inspired prayers today, you have the same invitation to an amazing life in the Spirit— seeing God's kingdom made manifest in your own life as well as in the lives of those around you—receiving wisdom and favor to solve financial problems; seeing spiritual, mental, and physical healing take over depression, illness, and disease; finding new purpose and fulfillment; solidifying and strengthening families; and so much more that the Bible promises to those who live in Christ. It is time to start living inside out, letting the goodness and love of God well up to the point of overflowing in all aspects of your life.

PRAYING EPHESIANS 3:14-21 FOR YOURSELF

Father,

In the name of Jesus, I praise and thank You that You saved me for a purpose, and that You have a plan for my life that exceeds my most imaginative hopes and dreams. For that reason, Father, I bow my knee to You, the God of heaven and earth from whom Your whole family receives our name. I pray that by Your glorious riches You would strengthen me on the inside through the power of Your Holy Spirit. Cause Christ to truly live in my heart and live through me by my faith in You. I pray that I would be able to understand with all of the saints the breadth, length, depth, and height of Your love which surpasses all knowledge. Fill me with all of Your fullness—Your wisdom, strength, power, and all—so that I would live constantly to Your glory!

Now unto You, Father, who is able to do exceedingly far above all that I ask or can imagine, be the glory in the church through Christ Jesus throughout all the ages and forever.

Amen.

PRAYING EPHESIANS 3:14-21 FOR OTHERS

Father,

In the name of Jesus, I praise and thank You that You saved _____ for a special purpose, and that you have a plan for _____ life that exceeds anything _____ has ever imagined or hoped for. For this reason, I bow my knee to You, the God from whom Your whole family in heaven and on earth have received our name. I pray that by Your glorious riches You would strengthen _____ on the inside through the power of Your Holy Spirit. Cause Christ to truly live in _____'s heart and live through _____ by faith in You. I pray that _____ would be able to understand with all of the saints the breadth, length, depth, and height of Your love which surpasses all knowledge. Fill _____ with all of Your fullness that Your wisdom, strength, power, and fullness would be in _____ to Your glory!

Now unto You, Father, who is able to do exceedingly far above all that any of us can ask or imagine, be the glory in the church through Christ Jesus throughout all the ages and forever.

Amen.

PAUL'S PRAYER IN CONTEXT THROUGH VARIOUS TRANSLATIONS

Ephesians 3:10—4:3 from the *New Living Translation* (NLT)

God's purpose was to show his wisdom in all its rich variety to all the rulers and authorities in the heavenly realms. They will see this when Jews and Gentiles are joined together in his church. This was his plan from all eternity, and it has now been carried out through Christ Jesus our Lord.

Because of Christ and our faith in him, we can now come fearlessly into God's presence, assured of his glad welcome. So please don't despair because of what they are doing to me here. It is for you that I am suffering, so you should feel honored and encouraged.

When I think of the wisdom and scope of God's plan, I fall to my knees and pray to the Father, the Creator of everything in heaven and on earth. I pray that from his glorious, unlimited resources he will give you mighty inner strength through his Holy Spirit. And I pray that Christ will be more and more at home in your hearts as you trust in him. May your roots go down deep into the soil of God's marvelous love. And may you have the power to understand, as all God's people should, how wide, how long, how high, and how deep his love really is. May you experience the love of Christ, though it is so great you will never fully understand it. Then you will be filled with the fullness of life and power that comes from God.

Now glory be to God! By his mighty power at work within us, he is able to accomplish infinitely more than we would ever dare to ask or hope. May he be given glory in the church and in Christ Jesus forever and ever through endless ages. Amen.

Therefore I, a prisoner for serving the Lord, beg you to lead a life worthy of your calling, for you have been called by God. Be humble and gentle. Be patient with each other, making allowance for each other's faults because of your love. Always keep yourselves united in the Holy Spirit, and bind yourselves together with peace.

Ephesians 3:10—4:3 from the *Contemporary English Version* (CEV)

Then God would use the church to show the powers and authorities in the spiritual world that he has many different kinds of wisdom.

God did this according to his eternal plan. And he was able to do what he had planned because of all that Christ Jesus our Lord had done. Christ now gives us courage and confidence, so that we can come to God by faith. That's why you should not be discouraged when I suffer for you. After all, it will bring honor to you.

I kneel in prayer to the Father. All beings in heaven and on earth receive their life from him. God is wonderful and glorious. I pray that his Spirit will make you become strong followers and that Christ will live in your hearts because of your faith. Stand firm and be deeply rooted in his love. I pray that you and all of God's people will understand what is called wide or long or high or deep. I want to know all about Christ's love, although it is too wonderful to be measured. Then your lives will be filled with all that God is.

I pray that Christ Jesus and the church will forever bring praise to God. His power at work in us can do far more than we dare ask or imagine. Amen.

As a prisoner of the Lord, I beg you to live in a way that is worthy of the people God has chosen to be his own. Always be humble and gentle. Patiently put up with each other and love each other. Try your best to let God's Spirit keep your hearts united. Do this by living at peace.

Ephesians 3:10—4:3 from the *Amplified Bible* (AMP)

[The purpose is] that through the church the complicated, many-sided wisdom of God in all its infinite variety and innumerable aspects might now be made known to the angelic rulers and authorities (principalities and powers) in the heavenly sphere.

This is in accordance with the terms of the eternal and timeless purpose which He has realized and carried into effect in [the person of] Christ Jesus our Lord,

In Whom, because of our faith in Him, we dare to have the boldness (courage and confidence) of free access (an unreserved approach to God with freedom and without fear).

So I ask you not to lose heart [not to faint or become despondent through fear] at what I am suffering in your behalf. [Rather glory in it] for it is an honor to you.

For this reason [seeing the greatness of this plan by which you are built together in Christ], I bow my knees before the Father of our Lord Jesus Christ,

For Whom every family in heaven and on earth is named [that Father from Whom all fatherhood takes its title and derives its name].

May He grant you out of the rich treasury of His glory to be strengthened and reinforced with mighty power in the inner man by the [Holy] Spirit [Himself indwelling your innermost being and personality].

May Christ through your faith [actually] dwell (settle down, abide, make His permanent home) in your hearts! Many you be rooted deep in love and founded securely on love,

That you may have the power and be strong to apprehend and grasp with all the saints [God's devoted people, the experience of that love] what is the breadth and length and height and depth [of it];

[That you may really come] to know [practically, through experience for yourselves] the love of Christ, which far surpasses mere knowledge [without experience]; that you may be filled [through all your being] unto all the fullness of God [may have the richest measure of the divine Presence, and become a body wholly filled and flooded with God Himself]!

Now to Him Who, by (in consequence of) the [action of His] power that is at work within us, is able to [carry out His purpose and] do superabundantly, far over and above all that we [dare] ask or think [infinitely beyond our highest prayers, desires, thoughts, hopes, or dreams]—

To Him be glory in the church and in Christ Jesus throughout all generations forever and ever. Amen (so be it).

I therefore, the prisoner for the Lord, appeal to and beg you to walk (lead a life) worthy of the [divine] calling to which you have been called [with behavior that is a credit to the summons to God's service.

Living as becomes you] with complete lowliness of mind (humility) and meekness (unselfishness, gentleness, mildness), with patience, bearing with one another and making allowances because you love one another.

Be eager and strive earnestly to guard and keep the harmony and oneness of [and produced by] the Spirit in the binding power of peace.

chapter *three*

GROWING IN WISDOM AND DISCERNMENT

This is my prayer: that your love may abound more and more in
knowledge and depth of insight, so that you may be able to
discern what is best and may be pure and blameless until the day
of Christ, filled with the fruit of righteousness that comes
through Jesus Christ—to the glory and praise of God.

Philippians 1:9-11 NIV

What could you accomplish if you always knew the right thing to
do? If you always knew how to correctly interpret information you
were given? If you always knew the truth, knew what was right, and
knew how to act upon it?

In our world today there are a lot of people who think that they are
always right. People speak with sincere passion and conviction about
what they believe in—and yet they can be wrong. The evidence they
base their convictions on could be incomplete or incorrect—or, at the
very least, misleading. Perhaps they had an experience that shot their
emotional-feedback meter through the roof so they could never deal
rationally with a particular issue. Or they became legalistic in their
thinking, using a set of rules and principles to make decisions until,
over time, their thinking becomes habitual and deceived. They are
increasingly convinced of the integrity of their conviction, even though
they are grievously wrong—sometimes dead wrong. Or they might
simply hold a conviction that gives justification to the way they live. It

is not a matter of truth as much as a worldview built to satisfy selfishness and carnality.

Paul knew the law of God. He had the best religious teachers available to guide his learning and thinking. He was zealous beyond measure for the cause of God. And as a result, he traveled the land imprisoning and killing Christians. He was sure he was right. He knew it in every corner of his being. And then he met Jesus—and his world was turned upside down.

What can seem so right can really be so wrong—until you meet Jesus.

But what happens when a believer becomes deceived? What happens when someone who has come to know Jesus falls back on the simplicity of following do's and don'ts rather than going from meeting Jesus to experiencing Him as a living, breathing Lord, Savior, and Friend?

How do you keep from slipping from a real relationship with Jesus to an artificial one? How do you go from that moment of euphoria of knowing in your heart beyond knowing that God is real and that He loves you to living a life of legalism so dead you are now questioning what God is doing in your life and in the lives of others? Once salt has lost its saltiness, what use is it?

STAYING ON THE RIGHT COURSE

In his prayer for the Philippians, Paul prays specifically that they would never lose their first love and wander from the true cause of Christ. Paul was writing to them from prison. Did some in Philippi now doubt what he had taught them because he was seen as a criminal? Persecution was on the rise—was it time to look back at the decisions they had made for Christ when Paul was there and determine now if they'd been misled? "Christians" were now coming from Jerusalem with new revelations about righteousness revealed through the laws of the Jewish prophets—shouldn't the words of such "godly" men be accepted over that of a man in prison and on trial for his life? What about different customs and traditions that were now arising for the "right" way to worship God? Shouldn't these be followed in order to grow closer to God just as so many others seemed to have experienced, rather than blindly relying on the words of a man in jail?

For any with such questions, Paul simply and clearly prays that:

(a) *Your love may abound more and more*
   i. *In knowledge*
   ii. *In depth of insight*

(b) *You may be able to discern what is best.*

(c) *You may be pure and blameless until the day of Christ, and*

(d) *Your lifestyle, conduct, and accomplishments can be "to the constant glory and praise of God."*

(*vv. 9-11* PARAPHRASED)

Paul prays for a balance in the lives of the Philippian saints so they can discern the truth and know how to correctly respond. For this, Paul asks God to give them three guides to help them always do the best thing: 1) the love of God, 2) true knowledge, and 3) insight from the Holy Spirit.

TRIANGULATING YOUR TRUE COURSE

Paul starts with praying for their love to increase and abound. Of the three guides, this is the one that provides motivation and action. There are a lot of people in the church today with tremendous knowledge of God's Word or about issues that are key to all of us, and others who have tremendous spiritual insight into matters of expanding God's kingdom on the earth, but far too few are really doing enough good to change things. Just as great trust and faith in God is wonderful, without love, it is nothing. (See 1 Corinthians 13:1-8.) It is love that moves our hearts in the first place to do something to help someone else, but it is a combination of knowledge and spiritual insight that gives us the wisdom to know the best way to truly help that person.

Throughout the Gospels we see numerous times where Jesus was moved by compassion to help others—He constantly had the ability to help and the knowledge of how best to do it—but had compassion not moved Him, the lives of those people would never have been affected. In fact, if it were not for the love of God, none of us would even exist, let alone be saved! For it was for the sake of love that God created us, and it was because "God so loved the world, that he gave his only begotten Son" (John 3:16).

On the other hand, love without knowledge and spiritual discernment is often ill spent. A loving, open heart is often more easily duped. It is, in fact, due to the good will for others that false charitable organizations prosper. They collect money for world hunger and other worthy causes, but then spend it on themselves. A savvy giver does not fall prey to these shysters. They carefully investigate the recipients of their giving, adding knowledge to their loving gesture. In other cases, justice that would bring repentance is too often derailed because human love gets in the way of the love of God—a parent indulges a child or a spouse enables aberrant behavior. When knowledge is added to love, we can respond appropriately for the long-term good of the person we love.

In the same way, correction without love—rules without relation-ship—can instill more rebellion than repentance because of dispropor-tional strictness or punishment. Any one of these three, without the other two, is prone to error—but when all three are working together, the will of God is accomplished with excellence.

GODLY EXCELLENCE

In the next three requests of this prayer, we see that each builds upon the other to the glory of God through our lifestyles and achievements. The first is that by correctly following the three guides of love, knowl-edge, and discernment we would be on the right path at all times and experiencing excellence in all that we do.

The true love of God is not just looking to bless others as a way of easing conscience, but as a way of life. It is not only a desire to bless but also to bless in the very best possible way. This would be true not only for blessing the hungry and orphans of another country, but as a way to walk through our daily lives—blessing our spouses, our friends, our children, our coworkers, as well as others who attend our church and also their families. As a result of wanting to be the best blessing possible, we seek to live and show God's excellence. We don't simply do enough to get by, we "go the extra mile." In the process, our best gets continually better. Our employers thrive because of our performance at work, our children and spouses grow because we work hard to keep those relationships strong, and hopefully our churches sparkle because they reflect the love of God we have for all who attend or visit there.

And again, this love must be coupled with knowledge of the things we are trying to accomplish or spiritual insight to set priorities—what we are to do and how and when we are to do it. It is heart, mind, and spirit all working together. And then as a result of growth and excellence in these three, the outside world looks at us and is attracted by the excellence they see. But Paul seems to think there are two more things we need to add to our outward excellence.

BECOMING AS EXCELLENT ON THE INSIDE AS THE OUTSIDE

It is not uncommon for a person to walk into a beautiful church and spend the first few minutes looking around at the architecture, the way the entry is decorated and arranged, noticing the cleanliness of the facility, and the way the people mingling there are dressed and how they talk with one another. They stand there for a moment, one step inside the doorway, taking it all in. They like what they see; they are impressed. But unless they find something deeper, something more lasting, they will soon disappear. A beautiful physical space will not keep them. Is excellence really exemplified on the inside? A beautiful exterior invites people to come inside. But are the inner qualities of the church as beautiful as its outer appearance?

It is one thing to do the right thing; it is another to do it for the right reasons. Appearances, as we all know, can be deceiving. And, unfortunately, we live in a world that thrives on appearance. Madison Avenue and Hollywood use beautiful people who are too often empty or corrupt on the inside to work their magic of illusion on us for their own purposes. Politicians and corporations carefully craft how they appear to the public—often while practicing dishonesty in their day-to-day practices. Edwin Louis Cole used to say, "The thicker the veneer— the cheaper the material." In the same way that good, quality wood doesn't need a thick glossy coating on it to hide its flaws, holy fruitful people should not need to hide behind artificial and contrived "fronts" to attract others. We should be as beautiful on the inside as we are on the outside.

Paul is praying that the excellence on the outside would be backed up by a sincere and blameless life bountiful in the fruits of righteousness.

TO THE PRAISE AND GLORY OF GOD

Paul is describing a life full of excellence in this prayer that simply starts by learning to do the right thing on a regular basis. He prays that we will be motivated by a growing love of God in our hearts that is counseled by knowledge from the Word of God and natural wisdom. He also prays that our consciences will be counseled as the Holy Spirit speaks to us. He prays that in this way we will show excellence to the world in both our outward performance and appearance, as well as showing forth a genuineness and blamelessness in all that we do. We should also demonstrate overflowing fruits of righteousness through Christ Jesus and thus be a tremendous blessing to others that will ultimately give glory and praise to God.

What a great thing for Paul to pray from within a prison cell! Yet at the same time, there may never have been a life that more fully exemplified this kind of prayer, nor an epistle that expressed more joy, proving that such a prayer can indeed be answered. It is time that more of us "volunteered" to be an answer to that prayer as well—by meditating upon it and praying it faithfully until it begins to manifest in our lives and spills over into the lives of those around us. God's excellence is there for us to walk in; we need only follow these three guides to truly live it.

PRAYING PHILIPPIANS 1:9-11 FOR YOURSELF

Father,

In the name of Jesus, I pray that Your love that was shed abroad in my heart by the Holy Spirit would abound and grow more and more, to the strengthening of my knowledge of You and of the things You have called me to do as well as in the discernment and spiritual insight of the Holy Spirit.

Help me to know the right things to do and how to do them with excellence, and to remain sincere, genuine, and real in all my encounters with others and free from blame or even the appearance of evil until the day of Jesus Christ's return. I pray that I will overflow in the fruits of Your righteousness, which I have because of Jesus Christ. Please cause all of this to make me a constant glory and praise to You under all circumstances and in all things.

Amen.

PRAYING PHILIPPIANS 1:9-11 FOR OTHERS

Father,

In the name of Jesus, I pray that Your love grows and abounds more and more in _____ in both knowledge of You and concerning the things you have called _____ to do, as well as in the discernment and insight of the Holy Spirit.

From this love, knowledge, and insight, help _____ to prove the excellence of Your ways and of knowing You. I pray that _____ might always be sincere, genuine, and real to others on Your behalf, and that no one will ever be able to find any reason for blame in _____ until the day of Jesus Christ's return. Cause _____ to overflow in the fruits of Your righteousness, which _____ has because of Jesus Christ.

All these things I pray that You may be glorified through the lifestyle and accomplishments of _____ and that _____'s life would be a constant source of praise to Your name.

Amen.

PAUL'S PRAYER IN CONTEXT THROUGH VARIOUS TRANSLATIONS

Philippians 1:3-11 from the *International Standard Version* (ISV)

I thank my God every time I remember you, always praying with joy in every one of my prayers for all of you because of your partnership in the gospel from the first day until now. I am convinced of this, that the one who began a good work among you will bring it to completion by the day of Christ Jesus. For it is only right for me to think this way about all of you, because I have you in my heart. Both in my imprisonment and in the defense and confirmation of the gospel, all of you are partners with me in grace. For God is my witness how much I long for all of you with the compassion of Christ Jesus.

And this is my prayer, that your love will keep on growing more and more in full knowledge and perfect insight, so that you may be able to determine what is best and may be pure and blameless until the day of Christ, having been filled with the fruit of righteousness that comes through Jesus Christ to the glory and praise of God.

Philippians 1:3-11 from the *Contemporary English Version* (CEV)

Every time I think of you, I thank my God. And whenever I mention you in my prayers, it makes me happy. This is because you have taken part with me in spreading the good news from the first day you heard about it. God is the one who began this good work in you, and I am certain that he won't stop before it is complete on the day that Christ Jesus returns.

You have a special place in my heart. So it is only natural for me to feel the way I do. All of you have helped in the work that God has given me, as I defend the good news and tell about it here in jail. God himself knows how much I want to see you. He knows that I care for you in the same way that Christ Jesus does.

I pray that your love will keep on growing and that you will fully know and understand how to make the right choices. Then you will still be pure and innocent when Christ returns. And until that day, Jesus Christ will keep you busy doing good deeds that bring glory and praise to God.

Philippians 1:3-11 from the *Good News Translation* (GNT)

I thank my God for you every time I think of you; and every time I pray for you all, I pray with joy because of the way in which you have helped me in the work of the gospel from the very first day until now. And so I am sure that God, who began this good work in you, will carry it on until it is finished on the Day of Christ Jesus. You are always in my heart! And so it is only right for me to feel as I do about you. For you have all shared with me in this privilege that God has given me, both now that I am in prison and also while I was free to defend the gospel and establish it firmly. God is my witness that I tell the truth when I say that my deep feeling for you all comes from the heart of Christ Jesus himself.

I pray that your love will keep on growing more and more, together with true knowledge and perfect judgment, so that you will be able to choose what is best. Then you will be free from all impurity and blame on the Day of Christ. Your lives will be filled with the truly good qualities which only Jesus Christ can produce, for the glory and praise of God.

Philippians 1:3-11 from the *Amplified Bible* (AMP)

I thank my God in all my remembrance of you.

In every prayer of mine I always make my entreaty and petition for you all with joy (delight).

[I thank my God] for your fellowship (your sympathetic cooperation and contributions and partnership) in advancing the good news (the Gospel) from the first day [you heard it] until now.

And I am convinced and sure of this very thing, that He Who began a good work in you will continue until the day of Jesus Christ [right up to the time of His return], developing [that good work] and perfecting and bringing it to full completion in you.

It is right and appropriate for me to have this confidence and feel this way about you all, because you have me in your heart and I hold you in my heart as partakers and sharers, one and all with me, of grace (God's unmerited favor and spiritual blessing). [This is true] both when I am shut up in prison and when I am out in the defense and confirmation of the good news (the Gospel).

For God is my witness how I long for and pursue you all with love, in the tender mercy of Christ Jesus [Himself]!

And this I pray: that your love may abound yet more and more and extend to its fullest development in knowledge and all keen insight [that your love may display itself in greater depth of acquaintance and more comprehensive discernment],

So that you may surely learn to sense what is vital, and approve and prize what is excellent and of real value [recognizing the highest and the best, and distinguishing the moral differences], and that you may be untainted and pure and unerring and blameless [so that with hearts sincere and certain and unsullied, you may approach] the day of Christ [not stumbling nor causing others to stumble].

May you abound in and be filled with the fruits of righteousness (of right standing with God and right doing) which come through Jesus Christ (the Anointed One), to the honor and praise of God [that His glory may be both manifested and recognized].

chapter four

WALKING IN THE PERFECT WILL OF GOD

For this cause we also, since the day we heard it, do not cease to
pray for you, and to desire that ye might be filled with the
knowledge of his will in all wisdom and spiritual understanding;
that ye might walk worthy of the Lord unto all pleasing, being
fruitful in every good work, and increasing in the knowledge of
God; strengthened with all might, according to his glorious
power, unto all patience and longsuffering with joyfulness;
giving thanks unto the Father, which hath made us meet to be
partakers of the inheritance of the saints in light.

Colossians 1:9-12

If you are praying for someone to grow, there is never a reason to
stop until they go home to be with their Lord and Savior. Thus, while
many of us focus on praying over the requests of those in trouble or in
need, Paul continually prays for the saints when he knows that they are
doing well. Paul's prayer is that they keep on going, keep on growing,
and keep on reaching new levels in Christ. Paul never acknowledges a
place where any of us can sit back and say we have arrived—there is so
much to God that there is an eternity awaiting us to get to know Him.
Yet how much more will His kingdom manifest on earth if we strive to
know Him fully here rather than waiting until heaven when that
knowledge will come too late to help other people?

Evangelism, praying for the sick, and other forms of outreach to nonbelievers is hard for the vast majority of the church. Such actions are frequently far outside of our comfort zones. While living a godly lifestyle is a great witness to the world, far too many of us use it as a crutch for never telling others around us of the wonders of knowing Jesus. Often, great opportunities come when someone asks, "What is it that is so different about you? You are always so at peace? Where does that peace come from?" However, this should be an added bonus to our ministry on the earth rather than the main thrust of it. The real key to evangelism is not waiting for others to ask, but waiting upon the Lord until the Holy Spirit gives us the right words as we step out. As the Proverb says "How good is a timely word!" (Proverbs 15:23 NIV). And if we will only trust in Him, He will give us exactly the right words for the right time in someone else's life.

However, such things are often hard for Christians because they have stopped their ardent pursuit to really know God as fully as possible. Look at "mature" believers whom you know: Are they more likely to share their faith or less? Are they more likely to take someone's hand and pray without concern for where they are or less likely? The truth of the matter is that the better we know God, the more natural these things become. Yes, there are those who do such things out of a sense of Christian duty, but there are others who simply know God and His love so well that it's natural for them to introduce others to their Friend who can help in any time of need.

This is why when Paul had "heard of your faith in Christ Jesus, and of the love which ye have to all the saints" (Colossians 1:4), it was not only an opportunity to praise and thank God for His faithfulness but also to pray for further growth. What would it mean for us to stand before the judgment seat of Christ and say, "I had Your faith and Your love, but I didn't fulfill the mission You called me to accomplish on earth. Your faith and Your love were enough, weren't they?"

This is why in the midst of his praise to God for the Colossians, Paul also springs into prayer for them: *It is because of your faith and love and this glorious Gospel that has been entrusted to us that I have not ceased to pray for you from the day I heard you were doing so well. Because of these things I ask God that:*

(a) *You would be filled with the knowledge of His will—both for your calling and in every situation and circumstance of life you experience—in both wisdom and understanding (both in principled application and spiritual insight).*

(b) *The walk you have in our Lord Jesus Christ would be to the fullness of all of His pleasure.*

(c) *You would be fruitful in every good deed and work.*

(d) *You would be continually increasing in the knowledge of God without ever, ever stopping;*

(e) *You can be strengthened with all might and conviction according to His glorious power to the point that you bear all things with a patience and longsuffering so steadfast that outwardly it appears only as joy that gives thanks to the Father.*

The Father is the One who has made us fit to partake of our inheritance in Jesus with all of the other saints in light, because it had always been His plan to save us through Jesus Christ.

—(Colossians 1:9-12 PARAPHRASED*)*

Paul's call here is that the Colossians would refuse to sit on their laurels and look at their accomplishments, thinking they had done enough to please God for today, and thus tomorrow they could "retire," sitting back to enjoy the fruit of their labors. His prayer is that they would push on into the full realization and accomplishment of what God called them to do, and that walking out His perfect will would come naturally for them as they learned to walk in the knowledge of Him and His Spirit. Since his desire and prayer would be the same for us as we prosper in the knowledge and will of God today, it is again worth looking more closely at these supplications to see how we might add them to our prayers for ourselves and others.

BEING FILLED WITH THE KNOWLEDGE OF HIS WILL IN BOTH WISDOM AND UNDERSTANDING

In Romans Paul describes our calling to fulfill all of God's will on earth:

> I beseech you therefore, brethren, by the mercies of God, that you present your bodies a living sacrifice, holy, acceptable to God, which is your reasonable service. And do not be conformed to this world, but be transformed by the renewing of your mind, that you may prove what is that good and acceptable and perfect will of God.
>
> —*Romans 12:1-2* NKJV

There is a problem with living sacrifices—they tend to keep crawling off the altar!

Thus Paul's call to present our bodies as living sacrifices to God—presenting our hands and feet as well as our eyes, ears, and mouths—is a daily, if not hourly, task. "Here is my body, Father, to do the tasks You want me to do." And when it crawls off the altar, as we all know it will, we should not give up in frustration, but pick it up and throw it back up there. Note that God doesn't need a dead sacrifice, but a living one that can "live and move and be." (See Acts 17:28.) He needs action focused on making faith vibrant—not dry, dusty pride stuck in the accomplishments of the past.

Paul also calls for the "renewing of your mind" that you might change "your" way of thinking to "God's" way of thinking. When you are confronted with a situation, how do you react? Do you accept setbacks as "a way of life," or do you see them as "opportunities to see God's salvation?" Do you strive to appear efficient and loyal while abusing your position and privileges when the boss's back is turned? Do you spend your time to bolster your reputation and enjoy your hobbies to the detriment of your family or your relationship with God? Or are you doing well in the Lord, growing in God, balancing your work, family, and other areas of your life appropriately? We all need to grow more in thinking as God thinks rather than letting our minds lapse into the patterns of thought set forth by the world around us. Only then can we recognize and prove as true the good, acceptable, and perfect will of God.

This amplifies why Paul prays that the Colossians "would be filled with the knowledge of His will in all wisdom and spiritual understanding." To know God's will is to see it like the blueprint of a house laid out before us. Here is the plan—the *will* of the Designer.

Yet here Paul is not just talking of the hope of our callings in Christ as he prayed for in Ephesians 1 but also that we would know the will of God in any circumstance we encounter. Too many Christians come to a difficult situation in their lives or that of someone they know and pray, "Lord, Thy will be done," as if that will is some mystery beyond human comprehension. Praying "Thy will be done" when you don't know what His will is does not agree with Scripture.

When Jesus prayed "Thy will be done, Father" in the Garden of Gethsemane, He *knew* what that will was. It was not a prayer of giving Himself up to the unknowable mystery of what God might be trying to teach Him through the Cross. Instead, he knew that God was calling Him to the Cross to save humanity and that it would be a hard thing to go through and endure. Yet, knowing it was His Father's perfect will, He would set His course to go through it in a manner that would glorify His Father. It was a prayer of consecration and dedication to the will of God, not a prayer of throwing His future into uncertainty.

When Paul decided to return to Jerusalem after his third missionary journey, he knew chains and imprisonment awaited him there, yet he also knew through many confirmations in the Spirit that it was God's will he be arrested in order to testify of the Gospel before magistrates and judges from Caesarea to Rome. God wasn't trying to teach Paul something through what he would suffer through incarceration and trials. He was using those things as an opportunity for Paul to testify to the Truth. God's will in any circumstance of life should be no mystery to any of us *in Christ*—and especially any of us who know the promises He's given us in His Word.

However, Paul does pray we would have knowledge of God's will alone. Again, it is one thing to know, it is another to act correctly. Thus

Paul's full prayer is that they would "be filled with the knowledge of God's will in all *wisdom* and spiritual *understanding*." Wisdom comes from the Word of God; understanding comes from the Spirit of God. Wisdom is the ability to apply knowledge correctly and effectively; understanding comprehends its purpose, intensity, and timing. With the knowledge of God's will in wisdom and understanding, you can plot your good, acceptable, and perfect course through the circumstances or difficulties of life because you know what lies on the other side as well as how to navigate by faith through the midst of seemingly insurmountable obstacles. As David said:

> Yea, though I walk *through* the valley of the shadow of death, I will fear no evil: for thou art with me; thy rod and thy staff they comfort me. Thou preparest a table before me *in the presence* of mine enemies: thou anointest my head with oil; my cup runneth over. Surely goodness and mercy shall follow me all the days of my life: and I will dwell in the house of the LORD for ever.
>
> —*Psalm 23:4-6* (emphasis added)

David speaks here not of being destroyed in the valley of the shadow of death, but of being preserved while passing *through* it. He knows that God promised something for him on the other side and that He would be with him through it all as a shepherd with his rod (a weapon for beating away enemies and predators) and his staff (a pole with a crook used to rescue and direct the sheep as needed). David also speaks of being seated in honor at a table that gathers all of his enemies into one place. No matter who opposes him and where they oppose him from, the Host of the dinner will see His guest honored and filled to overflowing so that goodness and mercy are his rewards, not death in the valley or any plot his enemies may have made against him.

For this same reason, God wants you to see His will with wisdom and understanding so you can clearly plot your way *through* to what He has for you on the other side—His promises.

WALKING WORTHY

The phrases "walking in love" or "walking in the Spirit" are most often thought to be references to the things we are doing regularly in our lives, thinking of it as a call to operate through the Spirit and God's love in every hour and minute of our days. The regularity, the consistency, the faithfulness exhibited in our daily lives is of great value. At the same time, we should not overlook the other important part of walking—*that it is aimed at getting someplace we want to be.*

In this light your walk is your journey from where you are now to where God has called you to be—it is ground you cover day after day toward accomplishing His goals, aspirations, hopes, and purposes in your life. Paul's prayer is that you "walk worthy of the Lord unto all pleasing." How are you seen by those you work with, those in your family, those you go to church with, and those you spend your time with? Do they see excellence or compromise? Do they see genuineness and integrity or corner cutting and selfishness?

And what about the things you do when no one is watching but God—in your private times, when you are away from home, when you think no one will ever find out. It is Paul's prayer that in all these things you will "please him in every way" (Colossians 1:10 NIV).

This is the "lifestyle evangelism" component of your walks on the earth. It is the integrity you live with. Outwardly it is your reputation, but privately it is the true source of your inner strength.

Have you ever thought about what the word *integrity* really means? Most people use it in the sense of "living a moral and principled life." But this must be moral and principled living that goes beyond the outward appearance and resides in your inner character. Only then will you be truly pleasing to God. Think of it this way. The "internal integrity" of a building, airplane, or car is what keeps it intact—even though no one can really see the inner framework of beams and joints—and protects those inside in case of stress induced by a calamity such as an earthquake or collision. It measures the purity of a substance and the soundness of a structure, and it is never truly tested until it is under duress or in a crisis.

Historical theorists have suggested that to cut costs on the *Titanic,* the iron rivets used to hold the side of the ship intact were mixed with cheaper materials, and the procedure used to make the side plates may have made them more brittle in the icy waters of the North Atlantic. For the first part of the trip, everything was smooth sailing. After the ship hit the iceberg, however, those rivets popped like corks out of champagne bottles and the steel plates tore because of their brittleness. These theories suggest that the "unsinkable" ship went to the bottom not so much because it struck an iceberg, but because it lacked internal integrity.[6]

True integrity does not come from what *is* seen as much as what *is not* seen. It is for this internal strength that Paul is praying when he requests you "live a life worthy of the Lord and may please him in every way" (Colossians 1:10 NIV).

BEING FRUITFUL

Fruitfulness has never been measured by potential. While a tree may have wonderful branches and great potential to bear fruit, it is not fruitful. Even if a tree has a large number of blossoms, it is still not fruitful. Nor is a tree fruitful that has young unripe fruit on its branches. A tree cannot be called fruitful until someone can pull the fruit off the stem, admire its health and freedom from pests, and take a bite of that fruit, benefiting from the nutrients locked up inside. And the fruit is not for the benefit of the tree; it is to nourish others with the life that flows through its branches and stems.

Paul prays that you would be "fruitful in every good work," feeding the world with the life of Christ flowing through your veins. He wants more for you than starting works or helping others from time to time before throwing in the towel and saying that's enough. God's plan is that you reach out and change your world from the planting of the seed of an idea to bringing that work to full fruitfulness on the vine. He wants His plans through you to touch your community in significant ways. As a member of the Body of Christ, you are a change-maker and a life-restorer through the power of God within you. While the spiritual fruit you bear—"love, joy, peace, patience, kindness, goodness, faithfulness, gentleness and self-control" (Galatians 5:22-23 NIV)—can be a tremendous blessing in your own life, it is intended to benefit others, allowing them to see Christ in you and come to a saving knowledge of the Truth.

KNOWING GOD

More than any other request, Paul prayed that we would "increase in the knowledge of God." He prayed it for the Ephesians, the

Philippians, and here again for the Colossians. These were three of the most mature and prospering churches he had planted, and yet for each he prays that their knowledge of God would increase. Why is this?

Peter was the one to state it most clearly:

> Grace and peace be multiplied to you *in the knowledge of God and of Jesus our Lord,* as His divine power has given to us all things that pertain to life and godliness, *through the knowledge of Him* who called us by glory and virtue, by which have been given to us exceedingly great and precious promises, that through these you may be partakers of the divine nature, having escaped the corruption that is in the world through lust.
>
> —*2 Peter 1:2-4* NKJV (emphasis added)

According to this passage, the knowledge of God gives us:

- All things that pertain to life.
- All things that pertain to godliness.
- Exceedingly great and precious promises.

All of this is so we can partake in His nature and escape the corruption that comes into our world through lust.

Most often, when we think of lust, we think of sexual lust, but the Bible often uses this term more broadly. In the parable of the "sower," Jesus tells us that fruitfulness in maturing Christians can be choked out by "the cares of this world, and the deceitfulness of riches, and the *lusts* of other things" (Mark 4:19 [emphasis added]). These things can grow in us like thorn bushes and keep our fruit from ever maturing to benefit others. In Romans, Paul calls this lust "coveting":

> What shall we say then? Is the law sin? God forbid. Nay, I had not known sin, but by the law: for I had not known lust, except the law had said, Thou shalt not covet.
>
> —*Romans 7:7*

In this sense, "lust" is referring to an inordinate desire for what belongs to others. The corruption that "is in the world through lust" is more simply the tendency to indulge selfish desires, especially at the expense of others. However, in truth, any indulgence that hinders the growth of spiritual fruit in our lives is at the expense of those who might someday have enjoyed the nourishment it provides. When we decrease our spiritual potency, we handicap those who depend on us.

However, as we grow to know God more fully, such "indulgences" become less a question of will power and more the reality of a changed nature. Why indulge lusts when we can find edification through our relationship with Christ? Certainly we all have drives and desires that need to be satisfied, but first they must be sanctified. Sex inside of a happy marriage is a blessing just as ambition toward God's plan and purpose for our lives is necessary, but each of these can lead to all kinds of problems when put to work in service of selfish desires.

Growing in the knowledge and fellowship of God is what keeps such desires in proper perspective. We escape the corruption that not only hinders God's kingdom on the earth but also rots our spiritual fruit on the branches. And just as trees must continue to grow and flourish through their seasons of life to remain fruitful, so we must continue to grow in the knowledge of God so that we can produce more and more fruit in each season of our lives—and touch more and more lives for Christ through that abundant fruitfulness.

STRENGTHENED WITH ALL MIGHT

This prayer in Colossians has many similarities to Paul's prayers for the Ephesians: in both he prays for our knowledge of Him to increase and an understanding of His will, as well as to be strengthened inside out with the might of God. Yet in this prayer, he adds another aspect to that spiritual strength. He prays that this strength would come through any situation of life with patience and perseverance exemplified by joyful praise and thanksgiving throughout.

Joy in the midst of difficult times is a miraculous sign of active faith. Take for example Paul and Silas in prison in Philippi. It would be easy in that circumstance to believe they had misspoken or had made a stupid mistake. Yet they knew through the Spirit of God (Paul's dream of a Macedonian calling Him to come there) that they were on the right track. So, rather than choosing depression and a "paralysis of analysis"—trying desperately to figure out where they had made a misstep—they glorified God and sang His praises *in joy* that they had served God worthily enough to invoke the devil's attention and wrath. They rejoiced that they were suffering for Christ's sake.

God wants that same joy to flow through you no matter what challenges, hardships, or problems you might be facing. For that to happen you need to have inner strength that only God can give. After all, the treasures of God's kingdom are different from those of the world for "the kingdom of God is ... righteousness, and peace, and joy in the

Holy Ghost" (Romans 14:17). Truly, what does the world have to offer compared to those?

FIT TO PARTAKE OF GOD'S INHERITANCE

Paul closes this prayer with praise to the Father of our Lord and Savior Jesus Christ because He "has qualified us to be partakers of the inheritance of the saints in the light" (Colossians 1:12 NKJV).

Again, Ephesians and Colossians are considered to be sister epistles in Paul's writings. They bear more similar themes and common phrases than any other two letters that Paul wrote. Yet the primary themes differ. Paul's letter to the Ephesians is the Church—the Body of Christ—and its function on the earth, while the theme of Colossians is the Head of that Body—the Lord Jesus Christ—and how we are to function in relationship to Him.

In closing this prayer, Paul refers to how God has made us fit to inherit His kingdom with the other saints and how we have been made fit to be joint heirs with Christ.

> He rescued us from the domain of darkness, and transferred us to the kingdom of His beloved Son, in whom we have redemption, the forgiveness of sins. He is the image of the invisible God, the firstborn of all creation. For by Him all things were created, both in the heavens and on earth, visible and invisible, whether thrones or dominions or rulers or authorities—all things have been created through Him and for Him. He is before all things, and in Him all things hold together. He is also head of the body, the church;

and He is the beginning, the firstborn from the dead,
so that He Himself will come to have first place in
everything. For it was the Father's good pleasure for all
the fullness to dwell in Him, and through Him to
reconcile all things to Himself, having made peace
through the blood of His cross; through Him, I say,
whether things on earth or things in heaven. And
although you were formerly alienated and hostile in
mind, engaged in evil deeds, yet He has now reconciled you in His fleshly body through death, in order
to present you before Him holy and blameless and
beyond reproach—if indeed you continue in the faith
firmly established and steadfast, and not moved away
from the hope of the gospel that you have heard,
which was proclaimed in all creation under heaven,
and of which I, Paul, was made a minister.

—*Colossians 1:13-23* NASB

What a mouthful! In closing this prayer, Paul launches into praise of
who God is and how Jesus accomplished God's plan for salvation by
His sacrifice on the Cross. All of this was so that you could be a
partaker of His inheritance, a joint heir with Christ, to the glory of
God the Father forever.

FINDING BALANCE

One of the most difficult things people face as they mature and move
toward their goals and aspirations is to achieve balance. As we have
already discussed, one of the devil's best strategies is to get us to focus

on only one part of the picture at the expense of all others. For example, if we are constantly focusing on our own problems, we will be of very little help to others. If we are spending all our time developing our ministry, we will not be the spouse, parent, or caring friend that we need to be. It's possible to be so into the work of the Lord that we forget about the Lord of the work.

Just as incorrect weights and balances in the marketplace lead to dishonesty and thievery, incorrect balance between all of the important realms of a person's life leads to faulty decision-making and poor judgment. Paul's prayer here in Colossians 1 calls for correct balance in our lives—the only true way of realizing God's full will, walking worthy of His pleasure, bringing His will to fruitfulness in our own lives as well as those of others, increasing in our knowledge of Him, and being strengthened spiritually by meeting all persecution and times of difficulty with joy and thanksgiving.

Perhaps to do that you will need to slow down in some areas to devote more time to others. The Puritans, for example, while they prized industry as a virtue, also felt that working more than your allotted hours for the day—thus taking away from time spent with God and family—was a greater sin than laziness. Living a balanced life may seem to cost you in some respects in the short run, but in the long run, you will be building a life rather than simply earning a living—a life full of godly fruit to share with others and becoming the blessing God has called you to be.

PRAYING COLOSSIANS 1:9-12 FOR YOURSELF

Father,

In the name of Jesus, I praise and thank You for Your faithfulness to continue the good work You began in me until that day You call me home to be with You. Because of this, Father, I ask that You further reveal to me the calling and purpose for my life, making it more and more real to me so I both know how to walk it out and have the spiritual insight into its timing and application; and that in every situation I would clearly see Your will and know how to pursue it effectively in order to fulfill Your perfect will for my life.

Cause each step I take in working out Your plan to be pleasing to You, Lord, and all of my efforts to overflow with fruitfulness. Cause each step I take to also increase my knowledge of You and help me grow closer to You.

I pray that I would continually grow in Your strength according to Your power to the point that nothing can phase me, and that I can endure anything that might come at me with joy and thanksgiving for what You have done for me, what You are currently doing, and what You are yet to do because, through Jesus, You have made me fit to take part in the inheritance laid up for all of the saints who walk in Your light.

Amen.

PRAYING COLOSSIANS 1:9-12 FOR OTHERS

Father,

In the name of Jesus, I praise and thank You for Your faithfulness to continue the good work you began in _____ until that day You call _____ home to be with You. Because of this, Father, I ask that You further reveal to _____ the calling and purpose for _____'s life, making it more and more real to _____ so _____ knows both how to walk it out and will see when and how to achieve it through the insight of the Holy Spirit; and that in every situation _____ would clearly see Your will and know how to pursue it effectively to fulfill Your perfect will for _____'s life.

Cause each step that _____ takes in working out Your plan to be pleasing to You, and all of _____'s efforts to overflow with fruitfulness. Cause each step _____ takes to also increase _____'s knowledge of You and help _____ grow closer to You.

I pray that _____ would be strengthened according to Your power to the point that nothing could discourage _____ so that _____ can endure anything that might come with joy and thanksgiving for all that You have done, all that You are currently doing, and all that You have yet to do because, through Jesus, You have made _____ fit to take part in the inheritance laid up for all of the saints who walk in Your light.

Amen.

PAUL'S PRAYER IN CONTEXT THROUGH VARIOUS TRANSLATIONS

Colossians 1:3-14 from the *New International Version* (NIV)

We always thank God, the Father of our Lord Jesus Christ, when we pray for you, because we have heard of your faith in Christ Jesus and of the love you have for all the saints—the faith and love that spring from the hope that is stored up for you in heaven and that you have already heard about in the word of truth, the gospel that has come to you. All over the world this gospel is bearing fruit and growing, just as it has been doing among you since the day you heard it and understood God's grace in all its truth. You learned it from Epaphras, our dear fellow servant, who is a faithful minister of Christ on our behalf, and who also told us of your love in the Spirit.

For this reason, since the day we heard about you, we have not stopped praying for you and asking God to fill you with the knowledge of his will through all spiritual wisdom and understanding. And we pray this in order that you may live a life worthy of the Lord and may please him in every way: bearing fruit in every good work, growing in the knowledge of God, being strengthened with all power according to his glorious might so that you may have great endurance and patience, and joyfully giving thanks to the Father, who has qualified you to share in the inheritance of the saints in the kingdom of light. For he has rescued us from the dominion of darkness and brought us into the kingdom of the Son he loves, in whom we have redemption, the forgiveness of sins.

Colossians 1:3-14 from *The Message* (THE MESSAGE)

Our prayers for you are always spilling over into thanksgivings. We can't quit thanking God our Father and Jesus our Messiah for you! We keep getting reports on your steady faith in Christ, our Jesus, and the love you continuously extend to all Christians. The lines of purpose in your lives never grow slack, tightly tied as they are to your future in heaven, kept taut by hope.

The Message is as true among you today as when you first heard it. It doesn't diminish or weaken over time. It's the same all over the world. The Message bears fruit and gets larger and stronger, just as it has in you. From the very first day you heard and recognized the truth of what God is doing, you've been hungry for more. It's as vigorous in you now as when you learned it from our friend and close associate Epaphras. He is one reliable worker for Christ! I could always depend on him. He's the one who told us how thoroughly love had been worked into your lives by the Spirit.

Be assured that from the first day we heard of you, we haven't stopped praying for you, asking God to give you wise minds and spirits attuned to his will, and so acquire a thorough understanding of the ways in which God works. We pray that you'll live well for the Master, making him proud of you as you work hard in his orchard. As you learn more and more how God works, you will learn how to do your work. We pray that you'll have the strength to stick it out over the long haul—not the grim strength of gritting your teeth but the glory-strength God gives. It is strength that endures the unendurable and spills over into joy, thanking the Father who makes us strong enough to take part in everything bright and beautiful that he has for us.

God rescued us from dead-end alleys and dark dungeons. He's set us up in the kingdom of the Son he loves so much, the Son who got us out of the pit we were in, got rid of the sins we were doomed to keep repeating.

Colossians 1:3-14 from the *New Living Translation* (NLT)

We always pray for you, and we give thanks to God the Father of our Lord Jesus Christ, for we have heard that you trust in Christ Jesus and that you love all of God's people. You do this because you are looking forward to the joys of heaven—as you have been ever since you first heard the truth of the Good News. This same Good News that came to you is going out all over the world. It is changing lives everywhere, just as it changed yours that very first day you heard and understood the truth about God's great kindness to sinners.

Epaphras, our much loved co-worker, was the one who brought you the Good News. He is Christ's faithful servant, and he is helping us in your place. He is the one who told us about the great love for others that the Holy Spirit has given you.

So we have continued praying for you ever since we first heard about you. We ask God to give you a complete understanding of what he wants to do in your lives, and we ask him to make you wise with spiritual wisdom. Then the way you live will always honor and please the Lord, and you will continually do good, kind things for others. All the while, you will learn to know God better and better.

We also pray that you will be strengthened with his glorious power so that you will have all the patience and endurance you need. May you be filled with joy, always thanking the Father, who has enabled you to share the inheritance that belongs to God's holy people, who live in the light. For he has rescued us from the one who rules in the kingdom of darkness, and he has brought us into the Kingdom of his dear Son. God has purchased our freedom with his blood and has forgiven all our sins.

chapter five

BIND US TOGETHER

The God of patience and consolation grant you to be
likeminded one toward another according to Christ Jesus:
That ye may with one mind and one mouth glorify God,
even the Father of our Lord Jesus Christ.
Romans 15:5-6

In the latter chapters of the book of Romans, Paul is dealing with a
very specific problem in the church in Rome. Since Christianity is a
universal religion bringing all humanity back to God—Jew and
Gentile; Greek, Roman, and "barbarian"; slave and free; king and
commoner; as well as every race, color, creed, and ethnicity on the
planet. With all of those various backgrounds and upbringings, how
would those Roman Christians ever see eye to eye enough to pray,
praise, work, and plan together to expand God's kingdom on the earth?
Could they function in unity despite their differences?

Rome was the New York City of its day, a hodgepodge of culture,
commerce, government, and art. People came from all over the known
world to settle there. At the same time, people from all of these various
backgrounds, races, and cultures were coming to Christ. How were
they to all tolerate one another enough to come together as one church
worshipping God and expanding His kingdom?

In Romans, chapter 13 through the first part of 15, Paul discusses
just what living by the law of love means. He discusses what duties

citizens have to their nation and then goes into a long discussion of serving custom versus conscience. Some said one day was holy, others said all days were equally holy; some refused to eat meat sacrificed to idols, others said whatever was sanctified by prayer was good for consumption. Paul summed it up this way:

> I know and am convinced by the Lord Jesus that there is nothing unclean of itself; but to him who considers anything to be unclean, to him it is unclean. Yet if your brother is grieved because of your food, you are no longer walking in love. Do not destroy with your food the one for whom Christ died. For the kingdom of God is not eating and drinking, but righteousness and peace and joy in the Holy Spirit.... Therefore let us pursue the things which make for peace and the things by which one may edify another.... We then who are strong ought to bear with the scruples of the weak, and not to please ourselves. Let each of us please his neighbor for his good, leading to edification.
>
> —*Romans 14:14-15, 17, 19; 15:1-2* NKJV

In this passage, Paul makes his strongest argument for de-emphasizing the minor issues of faith and customs of worship in favor of loving one another always with the goal of mutual edification.

We, too, should be willing to put aside the little things that are not of great importance for the sake of seeing others grow closer to Christ. The true issues are faith and honoring God, not particularly the manner in which these are practiced. We are to encourage one another to exercise the freedom available in Christ rather than adhere to religious bonds and meaningless traditions.

One of the drawbacks of religious practice is that too often it is used to control others—sadly this still happens today. The burden of legalism and creating one source of "truth" puts power and wealth in the hands of the religious leaders who control them. The Sadducees and Pharisees did this, as did the priests and priestesses of the "gods" of Rome. The Roman emperors were prime examples of this, claiming to be deity and demanding to be worshiped.

Today's cults and sects are formed under the premise that one person has received a special revelation from God that has never been given to anyone else. Soon that person would become the voice and guardian of that "special" revelation. Paul urges the Romans to distance themselves from those who enslave others and lead them away from the liberty available in Christ. One of his main problems, of course, was that believers from Jerusalem were trying to return Christians to the laws of the Old Testament and remove them from the freedom of life in the Spirit:

> Whatever things were written before were written for
> our learning, that we through the patience and
> comfort of the Scriptures might have hope.
>
> —*Romans 15:4* NKJV

From this point Paul then launches into prayer. In the process, he reveals the one true key to unity in the Church: *May the God of patience and encouragement grant all of you*

(a) *The will to operate with one mind and speak with one voice— acting and speaking with harmony according to who you are in Jesus Christ—*

*(b) Unity, through which you may glorify the God and Father of our
Lord Jesus.*

—(Romans 15:5-6 PARAPHRASED)

The key to unity is not disagreeing less, or even agreeing more—the
key to unity is each of us knowing who we are in Christ and acting in
accordance with that. The more we are like Jesus, the more we will be
in unity with one another. We won't be carbon copies of one another as
many religions and cults require—molding people to conform to their
standards of dress, speech, and behavior. Rather, we will be walking in
true unity, each part of the Body of Christ functioning to its fullest
capacity in obedience to Christ, the head.

Think about this as well for a moment. If we are to be similar in
thought, where is the brain of the body? It is in the head. And who is
the head of the Church? Jesus. So again, to be like-minded is to be
Christ-minded and Christ-directed. And then again, how did Jesus
speak? Where did He get His words of wisdom? "Whatever I say is just
what the Father has told me to say" (John 12:50 NIV). So if we are
going to speak in unity, it is not a matter of saying the same things, but
rather it is all of us saying what Jesus leads us to say.

Have you ever been studying the Bible and seen something truly
amazing that you had never seen or heard? If you are listening, you will
probably hear that same principle or insight from your preacher during
his sermon, a Sunday school teacher's lesson, the pages of a Christian
book, or from some other source within the Church. Unlike those who
hold that they alone have received a revelation, God's true revelations
come to many in the Body of Christ, ensuring their purity and
integrity and drawing us all together in unity.

WHY IS UNITY SO IMPORTANT?

Paul's desire for us to live in unity is crucial, clear, and echoed in Old Testament wisdom:

> Two are better than one, because they have a good
> reward for their labor. For if they fall, one will lift up
> his companion. But woe to him who is alone when he
> falls, for he has no one to help him up. Again, if two
> lie down together, they will keep warm; but how can
> one be warm alone? Though one may be overpowered
> by another, two can withstand him. And a threefold
> cord is not quickly broken.
>
> —*Ecclesiastes 4:9-12* NKJV

Separated, we are vulnerable to outside pressures, but together we are strong. We are to avoid divisions and work toward unity. As Jesus said, "If a house be divided against itself, that house cannot stand" (Mark 3:25). Division is perhaps the number one reason today that the Body of Christ is not as effective as God has called it to be.

Jesus acknowledged the importance of unity in Him when, on the night He was to be arrested and tried before being taken to the Cross, He prayed for His disciples and "for them also which shall believe on me through their word" (John 17:20). In that prayer, he prayed for our unity three times, but He never prayed more than once for anything else:

> I pray for them: I pray not for the world, but for them
> which thou hast given me.... Holy Father, keep
> through thine own name those whom thou hast given
> me, *that they may be one, as we are.... That they all
> may be one; as thou, Father, art in me, and I in thee,*

> *that they also may be one in us:* that the world may
> believe that thou hast sent me. And the glory which
> thou gavest me I have given them; *that they may be*
> *one, even as we are one: I in them, and thou in me, that*
> *they may be made perfect in one;* and that the world
> may know that thou hast sent me, and hast loved
> them, as thou hast loved me.
>
> —*John 17:9, 11, 21-23* (emphasis added)

When Christ spoke of forgiveness in Matthew 18—one of the very things needed to keep divisions from developing between Church members—He also immediately spoke of the power unity would make available to the Church:

> If *two of you shall agree* on earth as touching any thing
> that they shall ask, it shall be done for them of my
> Father which is in heaven. For where two or three are
> gathered together in my name, there am I in the midst
> of them.
>
> —*Matthew 18:19-20* (emphasis added)

It was also in times of Church unity in the book of Acts that God was able to move the most profoundly, as on the Day of Pentecost when the Holy Spirit was first sent to dwell on them:

> When the day of Pentecost was fully come, *they were*
> *all with one accord in one place.*
>
> —*Acts 2:1* (emphasis added)

In Acts 4:

> They lifted up their voice to God *with one accord....*
> And when they had prayed, the place was shaken
> where they were assembled together; and they were all
> filled with the Holy Ghost, and they spake the word
> of God with boldness.
>
> —*Acts 4:24, 31* (emphasis added)

And in Acts 13 when the Holy Spirit first called Paul to be a
missionary and an apostle:

> There were in the church that was at Antioch certain
> prophets and teachers....As they ministered to the
> Lord, and fasted, the Holy Ghost said, Separate me
> Barnabas and Saul for the work whereunto I have
> called them. And when they had fasted and prayed,
> and laid their hands on them, they sent them away.
>
> —*Acts 13:1-3*

Throughout his letters, Paul continually echoes the importance of
this unity. He paints one of the most beautiful pictures of how the
Body of Christ should work together to fulfill God's plans for the earth
in his letter to the Ephesians:

> I therefore, the prisoner of the Lord, beseech you that
> ye walk worthy of the vocation wherewith ye are
> called, with all lowliness and meekness, with longsuf-
> fering, forbearing one another in love; *Endeavoring to
> keep the unity of the Spirit in the bond of peace.* There is
> one body, and one Spirit, even as ye are called in one

hope of your calling; One Lord, one faith, one
baptism, One God and Father of all, who is above all,
and through all, and in you all. But unto every one of
us is given grace according to the measure of the gift
of Christ.… And he gave some, apostles; and some,
prophets; and some, evangelists; and some, pastors and
teachers; for the perfecting of the saints, for the work
of the ministry, for the edifying of the body of Christ:
Till we all come in the unity of the faith, and of the
knowledge of the Son of God, unto a perfect man,
unto the measure of the stature of the fulness of
Christ.… From whom *the whole body fitly joined
together and compacted by that which every joint suppli-
eth, according to the effectual working in the measure of
every part, maketh increase of the body unto the edifying
of itself in love.*

—*Ephesians 4:1-5, 11-13, 16* (emphasis added)

Like the parts of a body or a great machine, each member of Christ's
Church has a part to play in interaction with all of the others, and only
through each part working as it has been called can the whole body be
properly edified in love. As we saw in Paul's prayer in Ephesians 3, it
would be only "with all the saints" (Ephesians 3:18 NKJV) that the
surpassing power of God's love would be understood.

This picture of unity and function is one that has been lost by many
looking for ways to set themselves or their group above others. While
there are some points of salvation that are crucial to adhere to (such as
Jesus being divinely the Son of God), other preferences in how we
worship or the order of our services should not create barriers and

cause divisions between members of the Body of Christ. While we may prefer to "do things our own ways" in our individual meetings or services, that is no excuse for not standing together in prayer and action, as Pastor Ted Haggard in Colorado Springs says, "to make it hard for people to go to hell from our city." While there is a fight to be fought, it is not over minor points of doctrine as Paul pointed out, but between those who know God and the powers and principalities who would keep people from knowing God. The truth of the matter is that none of us can accomplish the will of God on our own.

On the subject of being like-minded, Paul also wrote:

> If there be therefore any consolation in Christ, if any comfort of love, if any fellowship of the Spirit, if any bowels and mercies, fulfill ye my joy, *that ye be like-minded, having the same love, being of one accord, of one mind.* Let nothing be done through strife or vainglory; but in lowliness of mind let each esteem other better than themselves.
>
> —*Philippians 2:1-3* (emphasis added)

Then later in the same chapter, Paul expresses why such like-mindedness is so difficult:

> I trust in the Lord Jesus to send Timotheus shortly unto you, that I also may be of good comfort, when I know your state. For I have no man likeminded, who will naturally care for your state. *For all seek their own, not the things which are Jesus Christ's.*
>
> —*Philippians 2:19-21* (emphasis added)

Division comes through selfishness; unity comes through seeking the things that are Christ's.

Paul saw this problem of division erupt in areas where he had established churches almost as fast as he could plant them. When he went on to start new works, legalists would follow him and take the freedom of new believers, who were learning to be led by the Holy Spirit, and return them to the bondage of life following the letter of the law. This divisiveness almost always led to the promotion of their personal ministries over the promotion of Christ's kingdom.

Where Paul planted unity and power in the Spirit, immediately Satan would be sent in to provoke those motivated more by selfishness than the love of God to steal its word, its unity, and its power through "a different gospel."

Today we see this same spirit of division everywhere to the extent it is dividing churches from one another, creating factions within churches, as well as dividing spouses, longtime friends, and families within the church to the point that those in the church look no different from those in the world.

In this prayer, Paul acknowledged that there are other virtues needed in order for those in the church to be able to work in unity. In verse 5, Paul calls the Father "the God of patience and consolation [encouragement (NASB)]." It is not hard to see why we need patience with one another if we are going to operate in unity, and Paul had just spent the last few chapters explaining that believers should encourage and edify one another rather than each judging the way the other seeks to honor God.

In effect, a key to living in unity is to always have the good of others in mind and to walk in patience as we work toward greater freedom in Christ.

TRUE UNITY

It has often been said, "If you have a vision that you can accomplish on your own, it's not from God." It is not God's desire that His Body on the earth work piecemeal to accomplish His will. We will never accomplish it all in that way. While each of us has a unique part, it is only when we connect and work in concert with others that God's perfect will can be made manifest.

That is why God is not just calling us to gather together and tolerate one another's differences, but to join our individual visions with those of others to encourage and work together, "So we, being many, are one body in Christ, and every one members one of another"(Romans 12:5).

As you find your place in Christ, you will see that it fits in with what others are doing as together God's common goals are being accomplished on the earth. When you and your brethren become one in Christ, all believers "may with one mind and one mouth glorify God." Add your voice to Paul's that true unity will come to the Body of Christ and that it will begin with one person—you!

PRAYING ROMANS 15:5-6 FOR YOURSELF

Heavenly Father,

I know that it is by Your Spirit that I have the power to forgive, and that it is through the fruit of Your Spirit that I can overcome

*the challenges of life and become an encouragement to others. I
thank You that You give me the power to be a unifier, a reconciler,
and a peacemaker so that others might see Your love and grace in
my everyday walk.*

*Therefore, Lord, I pray that You will use me to bring a spirit of
unity wherever I go and to whatever I do—at work, at church, in
my community, or even in my own family. I pray this so that with
one heart and one mouth we may all bring glory to You, the
Father of our Lord and Savior Jesus Christ.*

In Jesus' name. Amen

PRAYING ROMANS 15:5-6 FOR YOUR LOVED ONES, YOUR CHURCH, YOUR ORGANIZATION OR BUSINESS, OR YOUR CITY

Heavenly Father,

*I know that it is by Your Spirit that we have the power to forgive,
and that it is through the fruit of Your Spirit that we can overcome the challenges of life and become encouragers to others
around us. I thank You that You have called us as Christians to be
unifiers, reconcilers, and peacemakers on this earth as a display of
Your love and grace in our everyday walk. I also thank You that
You gave us an example of true unity in Your relationship with
Your Son, Jesus, as He walked upon this earth and that that unity
extends to us because of His prayers for us in John 17.*

*For this reason, Father, I pray for a spirit of unity for _____. I
pray that You would use _____ to be a unifier, reconciler, and
peacemaker, and that the Holy Spirit would be present with*

_____ *every day to help* _____ *overcome with Your joy and encourage others as* _____ *follows Jesus. I pray that in unity with one heart and one mouth* _____ *may glorify You, the Father of our Lord and Savior Jesus Christ.*

In Jesus' name. Amen

PAUL'S PRAYER IN CONTEXT THROUGH VARIOUS TRANSLATIONS

Romans 15:1-6 from the *New International Version* (NIV)

We who are strong ought to bear with the failings of the weak and not to please ourselves. Each of us should please his neighbor for his good, to build him up. For even Christ did not please himself but, as it is written: "The insults of those who insult you have fallen on me." For everything that was written in the past was written to teach us, so that through endurance and the encouragement of the Scriptures we might have hope.

May the God who gives endurance and encouragement give you a spirit of unity among yourselves as you follow Christ Jesus, so that with one heart and mouth you may glorify the God and Father of our Lord Jesus Christ.

Romans 15:1-6 from the *New Living Translation* (NLT)

We may know that these things make no difference, but we cannot just go ahead and do them to please ourselves. We must be considerate of the doubts and fears of those who think these things are wrong. We should please others. If we do what helps them, we will build them up in the Lord. For even

Christ didn't please himself. As the Scriptures say, "Those who insult you are also insulting me." Such things were written in the Scriptures long ago to teach us. They give us hope and encouragement as we wait patiently for God's promises.

May God, who gives this patience and encouragement, help you live in complete harmony with each other—each with the attitude of Christ Jesus toward the other. Then all of you can join together with one voice, giving praise and glory to God, the Father of our Lord Jesus Christ.

Romans 15:1-6 from *The Message* (THE MESSAGE)

Those of us who are strong and able in the faith need to step in and lend a hand to those who falter, and not just do what is most convenient for us. Strength is for service, not status. Each one of us needs to look after the good of the people around us, asking ourselves, "How can I help?"

That's exactly what Jesus did. He didn't make it easy for himself by avoiding people's troubles, but waded right in and helped out. "I took on the troubles of the troubled," is the way Scripture puts it. Even if it was written in Scripture long ago, you can be sure it's written for us. God wants the combination of his steady, constant calling and warm, personal counsel in Scripture to come to characterize us, keeping us alert for whatever he will do next. May our dependably steady and warmly personal God develop maturity in you so that you get along with each other as well as Jesus gets along with us all. Then we'll be a choir—not our voices only, but our very lives singing

in harmony in a stunning anthem to the God and Father of
our Master Jesus!

Romans 15:1-6 from the *International Standard Version* (ISV)

Now we who are strong ought to be patient with the weak-
nesses of those who are not strong and must stop pleasing
ourselves. Each of us must please our neighbor for the good
purpose of building him up. For even Christ did not please
himself. Instead, as it is written, "The insults of those who
insult you have fallen on me." For everything that was written
long ago was written for our instruction, so that we might have
hope through the endurance and encouragement that the
Scriptures give us.

Now may God, the source of endurance and encouragement,
allow you to live in harmony with each other as you follow
Christ Jesus, so that with one mind and one voice you might
glorify the God and Father of our Lord Jesus Christ.

chapter six

GIVE ME YOUR HOPE

The God of hope fill you with all joy and peace in believing, that
ye may abound in hope, through the power of the Holy Ghost.

Romans 15:13

As we begin looking at Paul's shorter prayers, it is important to
remember that God is not impressed so much by the length of a prayer
as by the faith that prayer expresses. It is easy to get caught up in the
eloquence and magnitude of Paul's prayers to the Ephesians,
Colossians, and Philippians and think his other prayers are not as
powerful, but that is not the case. They are just as important, and,
because of their shorter length, in many ways more useful. What would
it do for our "continually instant" prayer lives if the phrases of such
shorter prayers were so ingrained in us that we prayed them for others
every time we remembered someone?

Normally when we feel led to pray a short prayer for someone else, it
is basically just: "God, please bless _____." Instead we should pray
something like: "Father, direct _____'s heart into Your love and into
patient waiting for Christ. Comfort _____'s heart and establish _____
in every good word and work. I pray that _____ would increase and
abound in love for those in _____ family and church. Please, God of
peace, sanctify _____ wholly that _____ whole spirit, soul, and body
would be preserved blameless until the day of Christ."

Our prayer lives would almost certainly be more powerful if we were to pray such short prayers of faith regularly as the Holy Spirit leads us. Again, following the Spirit's leading in such prayers throughout our days—as well as longer ones when we have the time and feel so led—is exactly what Paul must have meant by his admonition to "pray without ceasing."

The better we understand the depth and meaning of these prayers—whether they be long or short—the more faith and understanding we can invest in them. And the more we understand them, the more faith they release. And the more faith we release in our prayers, the more they strengthen us as well as those we are praying for.

Thus Paul added this prayer for the Romans almost immediately after he offered up a prayer for their unity: "May the God of hope—the Creator and Provider of hope—fill you with joy and peace to the degree that you place your trust and faith in Him, that you may overflow in hope by the power of His Holy Spirit" (Romans 15:13 PARAPHRASED).

Imagine the confusion caused by the merging of so many cultures and traditions. Unity must have seemed like a hopeless dream. Paul's prayer spoke to the heart of the first thing they needed before they could resolve their differences—hope to jump-start their faith.

WITHOUT HOPE WE ARE LOST BEFORE WE BEGIN

Why is it so important for you to have hope in your heart? What difference does it make? And why is it that of all the things Paul prays for the Roman believers, he asks that God would fill them to overflowing with divine hope? Why hope? Why not faith? Why not love? Why would hope be the first thing on his mind? Do we need such hope as believers today? What is the purpose of such hope?

Perhaps the first clue comes in the prayer itself: Paul prays that the "God of hope" would fill them with joy and peace in proportion to their trust in Him, and in addition to this—and as a result of it—that He would overflow their lives with hope through the power of the Holy Spirit. Paul refers to God as "the God of hope," inferring that He is the *author* and *provider* of hope, that He created it and distributes it. Hope is a gift from God, and joy and peace are by-products of hope. Joy and peace are the fruit that grow on the branches; hope is part of the lifeblood that flows through the branches to make that fruit grow. For you to fulfill your purpose and divine calling, you will need God's hope working in your life before you will even take the first step toward accomplishing it!

Hope is crucial for the accomplishment of any endeavor. Without it, you will do nothing—literally. In fact, the lack of hope is at the base of every problem you face in your life—it is a paralysis that captures and entraps you, keeping you from accomplishing your divinely appointed purpose on the earth.

At its most basic, hopelessness keeps people from attempting anything they might dream to do: Consider the young man who is hopeless about making the sports team. He probably won't even try out, but if he does, he is likely to give a halfhearted effort on the court or out on the field. Consider the young woman who feels hopeless about pursuing her dream to be a singer. In the absence of hope, she probably won't even audition for the choir. The employee who has no hope of promotion will most likely give an inferior effort. Parents without hope of peace are likely to discipline their children inappropriately while in search of it.

How about you? What is that dream that God has placed in your heart? Without hope, your dream is dead before it starts. God may be calling, but without hope, you cannot answer.

It is important to ask the God of hope to give you His hope. Here's why: In the face of Satan's onslaught to steal, kill, and destroy you and your family, you need hope. In the face of the growing resistance and intolerance of Christianity in the world today, you need hope. And in the face of God's calling upon your life to spread the Gospel to friends and neighbors trapped in the self-indulgent atmosphere of our society, the first and foremost thing you need to stay on course is hope.

Hebrews 6:19 tells us that hope is a sure and steadfast anchor for our souls. If you have hope, you can stay steady as a rock and weather the storm (just as Paul did when he finally got his wish to sail for Rome!); without it, you are lost and adrift and subject to whatever direction the wind blows—or however you are tossed by the waves. You will need hope in the midst of the tests, trials, and persecutions that inevitably will challenge your life.

In fact, Paul even states that hope is a blessed outcome of tribulations, trials, and persecutions:

> We also exult in our tribulations, knowing that tribulation brings about perseverance; and perseverance, proven character; and proven character, hope; and hope does not disappoint, because the love of God has been poured out within our hearts through the Holy Spirit who was given to us.
>
> —*Romans 5:3-5* NASB

How do tribulations, trials, and persecutions lead you to hope? Well, for those who don't know Christ, they don't necessarily. Many who run into resistance on the path to their dreams and aspirations compromise or give up long before they fulfill them. But for those who have Christ's hope overflowing in their hearts, new persecutions and trials give them only new chances to see His salvation and deliverance, which deepens their faith. When trials and persecutions are endured and overcome, character is developed. The person becomes increasingly determined to do the right thing no matter what the circumstances, and that proven character helps that person cling to the eternal and not the temporary. The persecutions and trials will pass, but God will stand steadfast through it all. And so will you when you have hope and faith working in your life.

As James 1:2-3 (NIV) teaches us, "Consider it pure joy, my brothers, whenever you face trials of many kinds, because you know that the testing of your faith develops perseverance." So cling to Him as that solid Rock of your salvation. No matter what the world and Satan throw at you, remember that you have a great hope that will survive the attack and even overcome it by the power of God. And no matter what it looks like at the moment, you will never be disappointed by that hope. One day when God has seen you through it all yet one more time, you will be the one who is laughing, and those who scoffed and criticized you in the midst of the turmoil will recognize God's hand upon your life.

Remember, no one starts a journey they have no hope of finishing, but many with hope will finish journeys they had never imagined beginning. Whatever answer you are looking for from God begins with the hope of receiving that answer. Why not take the time right now to ask the God of all hope to give you His supernatural hope and fill you with the confident expectation that what He started in you He will fulfill in you? Ask Him, by the power of the Holy Spirit, to revive in you and your loved ones the dreams and desires He placed there to begin with, and to rekindle the passion for Him and His kingdom that once burned so brightly.

There is an adversary of your soul who is determined to steal and extinguish your hope so that you cannot fight the good fight of faith and fulfill God's purposes for your life. But the God of all hope wants to fill you with His joy and peace in believing, so that you will abound in hope and walk in victory. It is time to start praying and believing that hope is yours for the asking—because it is. Don't give up on your dream, and don't let go of your hope!

PRAYING ROMANS 15:13 FOR YOURSELF

Father,

In Jesus' name I give thanks that You are the God of hope and that by drawing near to You and coming to know You better each day, You are causing overflowing hope to grow in my heart so that I might experience the depths of Your peace and the height of Your joy, even as I learn to trust You more fully every day, by the power of the Holy Spirit.

Thank You, Lord, that the more I learn to trust in You, the more the Holy Spirit, by His power, opens the floodgates of Your hope into my life. I receive Your anointing of hope right now.

Amen

PRAYING ROMANS 15:13 FOR OTHERS

Father,

Thank you that the more _____ learns to trust in You, the more the Holy Spirit, by His power, opens the floodgates of Your hope into _____'s life. Please help _____ by giving _____ Your anointing of hope right now.

In Jesus' name I give thanks that You are the God of hope and that you long for _____ to know You and trust You more fully so that Your hope may abound in _____ life. I pray that You will draw _____ near to You, Lord, and that _____ will come to know You better and better each day. As _____ does, I thank You for causing overflowing hope to grow in _____ heart so that _____ may experience more and more of Your joy and peace.

Amen.

PAUL'S PRAYER IN CONTEXT THROUGH VARIOUS TRANSLATIONS

Romans 15:4, 13 from the *New American Standard Bible* (NASB)

Whatever was written in earlier times was written for our instruction, so that through perseverance and the encouragement of the Scriptures we might have hope....

Now may the God of hope fill you with all joy and peace in believing, so that you will abound in hope by the power of the Holy Spirit.

Romans 15:4, 13 from the *Contemporary English Version* (CEV)

The Scriptures were written to teach and encourage us by giving us hope....

I pray that God, who gives hope, will bless you with complete happiness and peace because of your faith. And may the power of the Holy Spirit fill you with hope.

Romans 15:4, 13 from the *Amplified Bible* (AMP)

Whatever was thus written in former days was written for our instruction, that by [our steadfast and patient] endurance and the encouragement [drawn] from the Scriptures we might hold fast to and cherish hope....

May the God of your hope so fill you with all joy and peace in believing [through the experience of your faith] that by the power of the Holy Spirit you may abound and be overflowing (bubbling over) with hope.

Romans 15:4, 13 from the *New Century Version* (NCV)

Everything that was written in the past was written to teach us. The Scriptures give us patience and encouragement so that we can have hope....

I pray that the God who gives hope will fill you with much joy and peace while you trust in him. Then your hope will over-flow by the power of the Holy Spirit.

chapter seven

ESTABLISH MY HEART IN YOUR LOVE

God himself and our Father, and our Lord Jesus Christ, direct
our way unto you. And the Lord make you to increase and
abound in love one toward another, and toward all men, even as
we do toward you: To the end he may stablish your hearts
unblameable in holiness before God, even our Father, at the
coming of our Lord Jesus Christ with all his saints.

1 Thessalonians 3:11-13

When Paul prayed, his prayers poured forth from the flow of what he
was writing about as well as from the heart of the Holy Spirit who was
writing through him. In this first letter to the church in Thessalonica—
which is believed by many scholars to be the first letter written by Paul
to be recorded in the Bible—Paul expresses his concern for their faith.
Paul was concerned that the persecutions, which forced his departure
from Thessalonica, had worn on them and caused them to lose faith.
He had sent Timothy to see how they were doing, and Timothy
returned with the news that not only were they doing well, but they
were also spreading the Gospel with zeal throughout Macedonia. Later
in the letter, Paul says this about the excellence of their love:

> As to the love of the brethren, you have no need for
> anyone to write to you, for you yourselves are taught

by God to love one another; for indeed you do practice
it toward all the brethren who are in all Macedonia.

—*1 Thessalonians 4:9-10* NASB

Here we see, once again, that Paul pauses to pray for them, not
because of their need or want, but in the midst of their worthy progress
and out of a desire to return to them again shortly: *I pray that God
himself, our Father, and our Lord Jesus Christ, smooth the path between us
so that we may soon return to you and may the Lord:*

(a) *Make you increase, abound, excel, and overflow in your love for
one another.*

(b) *Make your love increase for everyone else around you both in the
church there and outside of it, both in Thessalonica and throughout Macedonia, even as our love for you has grown.*

(c) *May establish and strengthen your hearts to be blameless and pure
in holiness before our Father God, whom we will see when our
Lord Jesus Christ returns for us with all the saints who have gone
home before us.*

—*(1 Thessalonians 3:11-13,* PARAPHRASED*)*

Even though they were doing much better than he had expected,
Paul prays for the continued growth of their love that they might be
even more secure in their faith and righteousness before God. This
seems to echo the sense that our Christian lives are truly pilgrimages—
or walks—and that there is no time during that journey when it is safe
to sit back and say, "Yes, finally, this is far enough," until we know we
have accomplished the purpose God has specifically planned for us on
the earth.

ABOUNDING IN LOVE

In 1 Corinthians 13, Paul says that love is the most powerful thing in the universe.

> [The love of God] bears all things, believes all things, hopes all things, endures all things. [This] love *never* fails.
>
> —*1 Corinthians 13:7-8* NKJV
> [inserts and emphasis added]

Why is love so important? Because love is the only spiritual muscle that motivates us to do the right things, in the right ways, for the right reasons, and at the right times. God's love "is the fulfillment of the law" (Romans 13:10 NIV)—it is the accomplisher of righteousness and holiness. Faith, in fact, works by love. (See Galatians 5:6.) It is the mark of the Christian life that is to set us apart from those in the world—as the song says, "They shall know we are Christians by our love." It is the sign of spiritual exuberance as opposed to inner deficiencies or a life crippled by deep personal hurts. It is also the vine from which all the other fruit grow—"joy, peace, patience, kindness, goodness, faithfulness, gentleness and self-control" (Galatians 5:22-23 NIV). Again, the Scriptures tell us, "Against such things there is no law" (v. 23 NIV).

Love is the only thing that moves us outside of ourselves to join with others or to help others. The need for this love is the magnetism that God uses to attract us—without it we feel the "God-sized hole" within us. It is also the glue that binds together the different joints, ligaments, bones, muscles, and organs of the Body of Christ into one effective unit, moving toward the fullness of Christ. (See Ephesians 4:16.) And it is the attraction that draws those outside of the Body to come in and find their proper place in the kingdom of God.

Paul tells us that we have no reason to ever be lacking in love, because:

> The love of God is shed abroad in our hearts by the Holy Ghost.
>
> —*Romans 5:5*

Paul prays that this love would increase and abound within them to the point that it overflows to both those within the Church and those outside the Church. Given all of this, it is easy to see why love is so important in their lives. However, the fact that Paul feels obliged to pray for it has a concerning downside. If he has to pray that it continue to grow when they are already excelling so much in this area, it means that love can diminish if it is not nurtured.

In Jesus' messages to the seven churches in Asia Minor and Macedonia at the beginning of the book of Revelation, He reprimands the church at Ephesus for this very reason:

> "I know your works, your labor, your patience, and that you cannot bear those who are evil. And you have tested those who say they are apostles and are not, and have found them liars; and you have persevered and have patience, and have labored for My name's sake and have not become weary. *Nevertheless I have this against you, that you have left your first love.* Remember therefore from where you have fallen; *repent and do the first works,* or else I will come to you quickly and remove your lampstand from its place—unless you repent."
>
> —*Revelation 2:2-5* NKJV (emphasis added)

Though they excelled in knowledge, discernment, and wisdom, they had forgotten the love that had brought them to Jesus in the first place. They had grown content—acknowledging truth intellectually rather than living it. They had come a good distance on the journey toward fulfilling their calling, but they had stopped to set up camp only partway there. Assuming that they were doing so much better than others—they knew so much more than the other churches and had so much more revelation—they must have reasoned that they could stop here and rest. Jesus' message, however, was clear, "I will come to you quickly and remove your lampstand from its place—*unless you repent.*"

The church in Laodicea ran into a similar problem because they'd grown lukewarm:

> "I know your works, that you are neither cold nor hot.
> I could wish you were cold or hot. So then, because
> you are lukewarm, and neither cold nor hot, I will
> vomit you out of My mouth. Because you say, 'I am
> rich, have become wealthy, and have need of
> nothing'—and do not know that you are wretched,
> miserable, poor, blind, and naked—I counsel you to
> buy from Me gold refined in the fire, that you may be
> rich; and white garments, that you may be clothed,
> that the shame of your nakedness may not be revealed;
> and anoint your eyes with eye salve, that you may see.
> As many as I love, I rebuke and chasten. Therefore be
> zealous and repent."
>
> —*Revelations 3:15-19* NKJV

The Laodiceans had grown complacent in their prosperity and had mistaken worldly wealth for true riches. This attitude threatened to keep them from accomplishing the calling Christ had for them. Yet Jesus still loved them and counseled them to repent and recover their zeal. Otherwise, they could easily have missed all that God had for them.

Jesus also warned that in the last days, others would also falter in this area:

> "Because lawlessness will abound, the love of many
> will grow cold."
> —*Matthew 24:12* NKJV

We must never take for granted what God has given us so freely. We need to fan it back into flame through meditation on the Word, prayer, and exercising the "spiritual muscle" that the love of God poured so bountifully into our hearts.

ESTABLISHED HEARTS

Why is it the spiritual muscle of love that Paul wanted to see so fit and fruitful? He wanted their hearts and ours to be established as blameless in holiness before God until the return of Jesus Christ. The Ephesians and the Laodiceans had let their love and zeal grow cool. Now they were in danger of becoming "unestablished," meaning that the place God had called them to would be given to someone else. Paul wanted them to be firmly founded in their faith through the active growth of their love.

In this sense as well, Paul is praying that their hearts would be so firmly rooted in love that they could never be separated from their faith, their mission, or their growth and progress toward holiness. And Paul is surely not praying for them for their sakes alone. The church in

Thessalonica was quickly proving itself to be a center of the expansion of the Gospel throughout Macedonia, Achaia, and "in every place your faith toward God has gone forth, so that we have no need to say anything" (1 Thessalonians 1:8 NASB). In other words, their evangelism was going so well that there was no need for Paul or his companions to go to the area and found new works—the Thessalonians were already doing it! Those whom he had been concerned with about losing their faith in his absence were instead thriving. What a confirmation that must have been to the power of the Gospel!

Continue to echo Paul's prayers for this abounding love for all those the Holy Spirit brings to mind as you go through your days that you might be established in and accomplish all He has called you to do and be. May His love in you abound more and more to overflowing!

PRAYING 1 THESSALONIANS 3:11-13 FOR YOURSELF

Father,

In the name of Jesus, I pray that You would increase to overflowing Your love shed abroad in my heart through the Holy Spirit toward other believers and those I encounter daily who have not yet come to know You.

May my heart be established in Your holiness, blameless before You unto the day Jesus returns to this earth with all of the saints who have gone on before.

Amen.

PRAYING 1 THESSALONIANS 3:11-13
FOR OTHERS

Father,

In the name of Jesus, I pray that You would increase to abounding the love shed abroad in _____'s heart through Your Holy Spirit toward other believers and those _____ encounters daily who have not yet come to know You.

May _____'s heart be established in Your holiness, blameless before You until the day Jesus returns to this earth with all of the saints who have gone on before.

Amen.

PAUL'S PRAYER IN CONTEXT THROUGH
VARIOUS TRANSLATIONS

1 Thessalonians 3:5-13 from the
New American Standard Bible (NASB)

For this reason, when I could endure it no longer, I also sent to find out about your faith, for fear that the tempter might have tempted you, and our labor would be in vain.

But now that Timothy has come to us from you, and has brought us good news of your faith and love, and that you always think kindly of us, longing to see us just as we also long to see you, for this reason, brethren, in all our distress and affliction we were comforted about you through your faith; for now we really live, if you stand firm in the Lord. For what thanks can we render to God for you in return for all the joy with which we rejoice before our God on your account, as we night and day keep praying most earnestly that we may see your face, and may complete what is lacking in your faith?

Now may our God and Father Himself and Jesus our Lord direct our way to you; and may the Lord cause you to increase and abound in love for one another, and for all people, just as we also do for you; so that He may establish your hearts without blame in holiness before our God and Father at the coming of our Lord Jesus with all His saints.

1 Thessalonians 3:5-13 from the *Contemporary English Version* (CEV)

At last, when I could not wait any longer, I sent Timothy to find out about your faith. I hoped that Satan had not tempted you and made all our work useless.

Timothy has come back from his visit with you and has told us about your faith and love. He also said that you always have happy memories of us and that you want to see us as much as we want to see you.

My friends, even though we have a lot of trouble and suffering, your faith makes us feel better about you. Your strong faith in the Lord is like a breath of new life. How can we possibly thank God enough for all the happiness you have brought us? Day and night we sincerely pray that we will see you again and help you to have an even stronger faith.

We pray that God our Father and our Lord Jesus will let us visit you. May the Lord make your love for each other and for everyone else grow by leaps and bounds. That's how our love for you has grown. And when our Lord comes with all of his people, I pray that he will make your hearts pure and innocent in the sight of God the Father.

1 Thessalonians 3:5-13 from the *Amplified Bible* (AMP)

That is the reason that, when I could bear [the suspense] no longer, I sent that I might learn [how you were standing the strain, and the endurance of] your faith, [for I was fearful] lest somehow the tempter had tempted you and our toil [among you should prove to] be fruitless and to no purpose.

But now that Timothy has just come back to us from [his visit to] you and has brought us the good news of [the steadfastness of] your faith and [the warmth of your] love, and [reported] how kindly you cherish a constant and affectionate remembrance of us [and that you are] longing to see us as we [are to see] you,

Brethren, for this reason, in [spite of all] our stress and crushing difficulties we have been filled with comfort and cheer about you [because of] your faith (the leaning of your whole personality on God in complete trust and confidence).

Because now we [really] live, if you stand [firm] in the Lord.

For what [adequate] thanksgiving can we render to God for you for all the gladness and delight which we enjoy for your sakes before our God?

[And we] continue to pray especially and with most intense earnestness night and day that we may see you face to face and mend and make good whatever may be imperfect and lacking in your faith.

Now may our God and Father Himself and our Lord Jesus Christ (the Messiah) guide our steps to you.

And may the Lord make you to increase and excel and overflow in love for one another and for all people, just as we also do for you,

So that He may strengthen and confirm and establish your hearts faultlessly pure and unblamable in holiness in the sight of our God and Father, at the coming of our Lord Jesus Christ (the Messiah) with all His saints (the holy and glorified people of God)! Amen, (so be it)!

chapter eight

LORD, MAKE ME HOLY

The very God of peace sanctify you wholly; and I pray God
your whole spirit and soul and body be preserved blameless
unto the coming of our Lord Jesus Christ. Faithful is he
that calleth you, who also will do it.
1 Thessalonians 5:23-24

The day you were born again, your spiritual passport changed. No
longer were you a citizen of the earth with an uncertain future in eternity, but a citizen of heaven, now living in a foreign, and sometimes
hostile, world. As it was said of Abraham when God called him out of
Ur to the Promised Land, he and his family "admitted openly that they
were foreigners and refugees on earth.... They are looking for a country
of their own" (Hebrews 11:13-14 GNT).

It's common to hear among immigrants to the United States who are
raising families here, "We would never do that in the home country.
We did things very differently there. These things meant something
there. Oh, I wish we could go back to the old country someday so you
could see." Even though their lives were now planted in the soil of a
new homeland, they have trouble forgetting the old.

We, who have our citizenship in eternal life, should no longer long
for the "old country." If we had been flourishing there, we never would
have left, just as immigrants would not have left their former homes if
they had been happy there. Still it's true that our old lives often call to

us. As those applying for American citizenship are required to swear off allegiance to their old nation before they can become citizens of this country, how much more should we forsake all allegiance to the desires of this world when we swear allegiance to our Lord Jesus Christ and become citizens of His kingdom?

When God calls us to sanctification and holiness, He is calling us to turn our backs on sin and worldly desires and pledge our allegiance to heaven instead. In so doing, we become foreigners in this world. Aliens. Should we stand out and act a little differently than the rest of the crowd if that is truly the case? Should people be able to see that something is a little different about us? Shouldn't we be set apart from the common crowd in many very noticeable ways?

In the closing verses of 1 Thessalonians, Paul prays a prayer for the total and complete sanctification of the Thessalonians that they might be set apart to the works of the kingdom of God rather than confined by the dictates of the world and culture they lived in: *May the God of Peace Himself sanctify you completely from the inside out, through and through (make you an uncommon standout in your world, holy, setting you apart for His purposes). I pray to God that your entire spirit, soul, and body be persevered secure, complete, blameless, and sound (fit for heavenly use) until our Lord and Savior Jesus Christ's return. Since He who calls you is faithful, he will also make your sanctification sure"* (1 Thessalonians 5:23-24, PARAPHRASED).

In exactly the same way, God has called you out of the will of this world and its god (See 2 Corinthians 4:4.) into lives lived by the light of heaven. Are you willing to live by this greater citizenship, or are you still trying to "fit in," in a world that scoffs at righteousness? Are you willing to leave your allegiance to the things of this world in the dust, and count it all as "loss compared to the surpassing greatness of knowing Christ Jesus"? (Philippians 3:8 NIV).

SET APART FOR HIS GOOD WORK

As we discussed in the last chapter, Paul had expected the worst for the Thessalonians, but he instead received word from Timothy that their faith was solid and their love growing. Indeed, they were even spreading the truth of Jesus Christ throughout the region. New churches must have been forming everywhere they went. Because of this good report, Paul commends them and thanks God for them, yet at the same time he warns of the complacency that can come in the midst of such success. His message, in essence, seems to be something along the line of, "You are doing so well, bless God! Yet now, in the midst of your accomplishments, you are in an even greater danger of falling into temptation than ever before! Now that you are something in God, how much more Satan would like to see you fail and take down the faith of those who have heard your message and believed your testimony. The damage your fall could do is greater than what you have achieved to date, so stay strong! Live for holiness! Don't let yourself lapse into complacency and ineffectiveness. Don't let yourselves become recaptured by the cultural norms surrounding you. Live even now as citizens of heaven!"

In Paul's own words earlier in 1 Thessalonians, he said:

> Brethren, we request and exhort you in the Lord Jesus, that as you received from us instruction as to how you ought to walk and please God (just as you actually do walk), *that you excel still more.* For you know what

commandments we gave you by the authority of the
Lord Jesus. *For this is the will of God, your sanctification.*
—*1 Thessalonians 4:1-3* NASB (emphasis added)

Paul clearly expresses his desire here that they press on in Christ to
their complete sanctification in Him. In the following verses, he goes
on to give an overall description of what that sanctified life should
look like:

> Abstain from sexual immorality; that each of you
> know how to possess his own vessel in sanctification
> and honor, not in lustful passion, like the Gentiles
> who do not know God; and that no man transgress
> and defraud his brother in the matter because the
> Lord is the avenger in all these things, just as we also
> told you before and solemnly warned you. For God
> has not called us for the purpose of impurity, but in
> sanctification. So, he who rejects this is not rejecting
> man but the God who gives His Holy Spirit to you.
>
> —*1 Thessalonians 4:3-8* NASB

Of all the things Paul could mention—greed, deceit, hatred, pride, or
the like—Paul hits a note for the Thessalonians that very much
resonates in our culture today. There is no question about it: sex sells.
For those in Thessalonica at the time of Paul's visits, sexual gratification
was the primary marketing strategy of the pagan temples, very much as
it was in Corinth (which is also likely the location from which Paul
wrote his two epistles to the Thessalonians).

Sexual activity with priests or priestesses in these temples was the
"spiritual" worship of the culture. In a society where such indulgence

was seen as the norm and practiced outside of God's design, there must have been great pressure to participate. Was it possible for a person in Thessalonica to walk through the main part of town and not at least get tempted a dozen times to entertain the fantasy of such acts? Or for the Thessalonian believers to be able to hold fast to the model God had given them—monogamous sex with one person for life, sanctified by the covenant and sacrament of marriage?

Christians today have the same challenges. Our culture seems to be obsessed with sexual innuendo. It permeates our advertising, literature, and entertainment. It comes to us on the Internet, sometimes without our permission. Day after day, night after night, we are bombarded with unwelcome images that corrupt our values and tempt us to act outside the will of God.

Such open and pervasive propaganda might cause some to believe these things are permissible. We may begin to ask ourselves as Eve did, "Did God really say we should not eat the fruit? Maybe He just wants us to miss out on something good!" But Jesus exposed sexual sin at its very root—in the mind:

> "You have heard that it was said to those of old, 'You shall not commit adultery.' But I say to you that whoever looks at a woman to lust for her has already committed adultery with her in his heart."
>
> —*Matthew 5:27-28* NKJV

Why does Paul emphasize this? Because even though what is done in private may never be exposed and harm our reputations (although it very often does), such "intimate" corruption does destroy our true spiritual walk and relationship with God. It is an open door for deception to creep in and slowly corrode our standards of faith like rust corrodes a sewer pipe to the point that what is inside—and should be unseen—begins to leak out. Inner strength is traded for an outer facade—we trade relationship with God for religious appearance—the very thing Jesus condemned the Pharisees and Sadducees for:

> "You are like whitewashed tombs which indeed appear beautiful outwardly, but inside are full of dead men's bones and all uncleanness. Even so you also outwardly appear righteous to men, but inside you are full of hypocrisy and lawlessness."
> —*Matthew 23:27-28* NKJV

The message is clear: We need to keep ourselves pure from the fixations and fantasies of sexual immorality in order to remain effective for God's kingdom!

PAUL'S SPIRITUAL "TO DO" LIST

Living a godly life is not so much about disciplining the flesh to avoid doing what is wrong as it is to live by the Spirit and be consumed with doing what is right. Consider Paul's list of spiritual dos and don'ts that lead to his prayer of sanctification for them:

> We request of you, brethren, that you appreciate those who diligently labor among you, and have charge over you in the Lord and give you instruction, and that you esteem them very highly in love because of their work. Live in peace with one another. We urge you, brethren, admonish the unruly, encourage the fainthearted, help

the weak, be patient with everyone. See that no one
repays another with evil for evil, but always seek after
that which is good for one another and for all people.
Rejoice always; pray without ceasing; in everything give
thanks; for this is God's will for you in Christ Jesus.
Do not quench the Spirit; do not despise prophetic
utterances. But examine everything carefully; hold fast
to that which is good; abstain from every form of evil.

—*1 Thessalonians 5:12-22* NASB

This list is about getting so caught up in the purpose God has for
your life that sin cannot ensnare you. When temptation comes, can
you say as Joseph did, "How then can I do this great wickedness, and
sin against God?" (Genesis 39:9). For him, sin was personal. It wasn't a
matter of his own pleasure as much as it was quenching the purpose of
God in his life and hurting his fellowship with Him. It just wasn't
worth separating himself from God—for how could he do such a thing
to his Friend?

Paul's list of admonitions here are pretty simple to understand:

1. **Appreciate your spiritual leaders**—A grateful heart is a heart
   open to receive more from God. When we appreciate the gifts
   God has given to us in those He has called to be our pastors,
   teachers, and leaders, it is much easier for God to impart the
   wisdom we need to live the blessed life He wants for us. God's
   pattern is that when we submit to spiritual leaders, He will use
   them to impart that wisdom to us. When we are bitter or
   angry with them, it is like slamming the door on God's blessings through them. Certainly we may have differences of opinions and conflicts from time to time, but it is up to us to

forgive and work difficulties through to reconciliation—otherwise we forfeit God's blessing through that person!

2. **Live in peace with one another; admonish the unruly, encourage the fainthearted, help the weak, be patient with everyone**—As we discussed in Paul's Romans' prayer for unity, God has not given any of us a dream so small that we can accomplish it by ourselves. There are parts of God we will never experience or grow to understand without other parts of the Body of Christ. That means living in peace with others in the Church. This also means sometimes confronting others about tough issues (not being a busybody, but being eager to see them blessed and grow), as well as building up those who are going through tough times so they will stay the course.

3. **Always overcome evil with good**—In the Old Covenant, we were told to extract an eye for an eye. Evil was confronted with evil. But today, we live under the New Covenant—a covenant of grace. Rather than exacting revenge, we are told to turn the other cheek when we are attacked. We are to bless those who curse us and forgive those who hurt us. Even our enemies are those whom Jesus shed His precious blood to redeem.

4. **Rejoice always**—Rejoicing is not a feeling, it is an action. We may not feel like rejoicing and praising God when things aren't going well. But that's why the Bible speaks of a "*sacrifice of praise*" (Hebrews 13:15). If we can put a smile on our faces and praise God in every circumstance, His strength will be there for us and there will be no circumstance we can't endure. "Many are the afflictions of the righteous, but the

LORD delivers him out of them all" (Psalm 34:19 NKJV). We never have an excuse not to rejoice!

5. **Pray without ceasing**—As we are "continually instant in prayer," there is never a time when we must deal with our problems alone. All we need to do is lay our troubles before the Lord in prayer! As we are reminded of others, we should pray for them as well. A person who is instant in prayer cannot be defeated!.

6. **In everything give thanks**—As with rejoicing, there is no situation in which we cannot thank God. We may not want to thank Him for the situation, but we can certainly thank Him for His promises!

7. **Do not quench the Spirit**—Be open for God's miracles and spiritual gifts at all times. Never try to silence something God is trying to say because you are embarrassed or fail to pray for someone when God prompts you to do so. When the Holy Spirit tells you to do something, do it!

8. **Examine everything carefully; hold fast to that which is good; abstain from every form of evil**—Even the things we think we are sure of need careful reexamination from time to time to reestablish them in our lives. We need to remain ever teachable and open to new evidence, even if it may challenge our stand. Truth often lies at the end of a road of looking at seemingly opposing facts—and without the analysis of both sides, we would never have found it as quickly or fully. We must be lovers of truth in all things if we are to honor the Truth himself!

With these clarifications and admonitions, Paul has shown the Thessalonians the pitfalls they need to avoid in order to live consecrated lives and also some of the dos that will make citizenship in God's kingdom so much more appealing than the greatest pleasures the world has to offer. God has so much more for us if we are living by His Spirit! He has called us to overflowing lives. Why would we want to live any other way?

SPIRIT, SOUL, AND BODY

Paul's prayer here in 1 Thessalonians 5:23 is for total consecration from the inside out—spirit, soul, and body. We've discussed the three-fold nature of human beings in some detail, but what is interesting to note here is that when we speak of these three aspects of a person, we usually list them in the opposite order—body, soul, and spirit—and often when people read this scripture they put them in that order without even realizing it. However, Paul's emphasis was on the spirit. He rightly discerned that it should be first—that it is the source of true strength and holiness.

Though Paul lists the body last, he doesn't disregard the body altogether—it, along with the spirit and the soul, needs to be sanctified. In fact, the book of Hebrews talks of the importance of sanctifying the body as believers come into maturity in Christ:

> Though by this time you ought to be teachers, you
> need someone to teach you again the first principles of
> the oracles of God; and you have come to need milk
> and not solid food. For everyone who partakes only of
> milk is unskilled in the word of righteousness, for he is

a babe. But solid food belongs to those who are of full age, that is, *those who by reason of use have their senses exercised to discern both good and evil.*

—*Hebrews 5:12-14* NKJV (emphasis added)

As we reach maturity from the inside out, we can grow to a point where even our physical senses will be able to discern the difference between right and wrong—sort of like the idea that is expressed in the statements, "Something just doesn't smell right," or "Something feels wrong about this."

It is God's desire that we all reach this level of maturity, and every believer is capable of reaching it. As it says in the last part of this prayer, "He who calls you is faithful, who also will do it" (1 Thessalonians 5:24 NKJV).

We have a new "home country" in Christ, and it is time to let its culture, beliefs, and practices take over our lives. Neither are we just waiting here to go home with Jesus—we are in training to live with Him in eternity. We have every right to live God's will "on earth as it is in heaven" (Matthew 6:10 NKJV). It is time we started praying and believing for it on a much more consistent basis.

PRAYING 1 THESSALONIANS 5:23-24 FOR YOURSELF

Father,

In the name of Jesus, I praise and thank You for being the God of Peace. I pray that You would sanctify me completely from my inner spirit to my outer actions, making my life stand out to others as an example of Your grace, mercy, love, and righteousness.

Father, help me to walk worthy of my heavenly citizenship even as Jesus has made me worthy through His sacrifice on the Cross.

I pray that my entire spirit, soul, and body would be sanctified and complete for the purpose to which You have called me. That I would live blamelessly, above reproach, and without any appearance of evil—fit for Your use in all things and ready to spread Your kingdom upon the earth until the return of Your Son, my Lord and Savior Jesus Christ.

Now unto You, who called me, be the glory for ever and ever, even as You will be faithful to walk out and make certain Your sanctification and will are fulfilled in my life.

Amen.

PRAYING 1 THESSALONIANS 5:23-24 FOR YOUR LOVED ONES

Father,

In the name of Jesus, I praise and thank You for being the God of Peace. I pray that You would sanctify _____ completely from _____ inner spirit to _____ outer actions, making _____'s life stand out to others as an example of Your grace, mercy, love, and righteousness. Father, I pray that _____ would walk worthy of Your heavenly calling for _____ and _____ citizenship in Your kingdom.

I pray that _____'s entire spirit, soul, and body be sanctified and complete for the purpose to which You have called _____. I also pray that _____ would live blamelessly, above reproach, and without any appearance of evil and would be fit for Your use in all things. That _____ would fervently spread Your kingdom upon the earth until the return of Your Son, our Lord and Savior Jesus Christ.

Now unto You, who called _____, be the glory for ever and ever, even as You will be faithful to walk out and make certain Your sanctification and will in _____'s life.

Amen.

PAUL'S PRAYER IN CONTEXT THROUGH VARIOUS TRANSLATIONS

1 Thessalonians 5:12-28 from *The Message* (THE MESSAGE)

THE WAY HE WANTS YOU TO LIVE

And now, friends, we ask you to honor those leaders who work so hard for you, who have been given the responsibility of urging and guiding you along in your obedience. Overwhelm them with appreciation and love!

Get along among yourselves, each of you doing your part. Our counsel is that you warn the freeloaders to get a move on. Gently encourage the stragglers, and reach out for the exhausted, pulling them to their feet. Be patient with each person, attentive to individual needs. And be careful that when you get on each other's nerves you don't snap at each other. Look for the best in each other, and always do your best to bring it out.

Be cheerful no matter what; pray all the time; thank God no matter what happens. This is the way God wants you who belong to Christ Jesus to live.

Don't suppress the Spirit, and don't stifle those who have a word from the Master. On the other hand, don't be gullible. Check out everything, and keep only what's good. Throw out anything tainted with evil.

May God himself, the God who makes everything holy and whole, make you holy and whole, put you together—spirit, soul, and body—and keep you fit for the coming of our Master, Jesus Christ. The One who called you is completely dependable. If he said it, he'll do it!

Friends, keep up your prayers for us. Greet all the Christians there with a holy embrace. And make sure this letter gets read to all the brothers and sisters. Don't leave anyone out.

The amazing grace of Jesus Christ be with you!

1 Thessalonians 5:12-28 from the *New Century Version* (NCV)

FINAL INSTRUCTIONS AND GREETINGS

Now, brothers and sisters, we ask you to appreciate those who work hard among you, who lead you in the Lord and teach you. Respect them with a very special love because of the work they do.

Live in peace with each other. We ask you, brothers and sisters, to warn those who do not work. Encourage the people who are afraid. Help those who are weak. Be patient with everyone. Be sure that no one pays back wrong for wrong, but always try to do what is good for each other and for all people.

Always be joyful. Pray continually, and give thanks whatever happens. That is what God wants for you in Christ Jesus.

Do not hold back the work of the Holy Spirit. Do not treat prophecy as if it were unimportant. But test everything. Keep what is good, and stay away from everything that is evil.

Now may God himself, the God of peace, make you pure, belonging only to him. May your whole self—spirit, soul, and body—be kept safe and without fault when our Lord Jesus Christ comes. You can trust the One who calls you to do that for you.

Brothers and sisters, pray for us.

Give each other a holy kiss when you meet. I tell you by the authority of the Lord to read this letter to all the believers.

The grace of our Lord Jesus Christ be with you.

1 Thessalonians 5:12-28 from the *Contemporary English Version* (CEV)

FINAL INSTRUCTIONS AND GREETINGS

My friends, we ask you to be thoughtful of your leaders who work hard and tell you how to live for the Lord. Show them great respect and love because of their work. Try to get along with each other. My friends, we beg you to warn anyone who isn't living right. Encourage anyone who feels left out, help all who are weak, and be patient with everyone. Don't be hateful to people, just because they are hateful to you. Rather, be good to each other and to everyone else.

Always be joyful and never stop praying. Whatever happens, keep thanking God because of Jesus Christ. This is what God wants you to do.

Don't turn away God's Spirit or ignore prophecies. Put everything to the test. Accept what is good and don't have anything to do with evil.

I pray that God, who gives peace, will make you completely holy. And may your spirit, soul, and body be kept healthy and faultless until our Lord Jesus Christ returns. The one who chose you can be trusted, and he will do this.

Friends, please pray for us.

Give the Lord's followers a warm greeting.

In the name of the Lord I beg you to read this letter to all his followers.

I pray that our Lord Jesus Christ will be kind to you!

chapter nine

FULFILL YOUR WHOLE PURPOSE IN ME

We pray always for you, that our God would count you worthy
of this calling, and fulfil all the good pleasure of his goodness,
and the work of faith with power: That the name of our Lord
Jesus Christ may be glorified in you, and ye in him, according
to the grace of our God and the Lord Jesus Christ.

2 Thessalonians 1:11-12

The church in Thessalonica was experiencing persecution on two
fronts: those who despised their faith for Christ's sake and false teachers
who had infiltrated the congregation. What was Paul's message to them
to help them stay strong through these pressures?

Jesus is coming again.

More than any other of his writings, the letters to the
Thessalonians—and especially 2 Thessalonians—talks of the second
coming of Jesus Christ and His imminent return for His own.

Yet Paul's point is not to opt out—looking beyond the difficulties
and the challenges of living, expecting Jesus to launch a "rescue"—but
that Jesus' imminent return should be a motivator to accomplish all the
more quickly the things God has called us to do on this earth. It was
not a message to look for deliverance in the midst of a losing battle,
but to win the war before time ran out—before our prize and crown of
victory were taken away by our own negligence to act when the time
was right. Certainly the enemy is mounting its offensive and trying to

scatter confusion within the ranks with false teachings—but don't let that set you back! This is not the time to wander aimlessly about. It is time to make those dreams and hopes in your heart come true! It is for this fight that God called you out of the world to live for His kingdom. Don't disappoint Him—and yourself—by coming up short.

This is why, in the process of encouraging the believers in Thessalonica to cling to the truth he had taught them, Paul also prays: *Because of your love, your faith, and your patience in the midst of persecutions and tribulations, and because our Lord Jesus Christ is coming again to be glorified among all who believe on His Gospel as you have, we— Timothy, Silvanus, and myself—all pray always for you that:*

> (a) *God will recognize you as worthy and enable you through His ability to accomplish the life's calling He has given you.*

> (b) *He would fulfill the good pleasure of His goodness in you, fulfilling by His power all of your desire for goodness and the good things you endeavor to accomplish.*

> (c) *You would complete the works to which you have set your faith through the power of God within you.*

> (d) *The name of our Lord Jesus Christ will receive glory from you.*

> (e) *You will have glory in Him as you stand strong and keep your hands to His plow. Now let all of this be done that glory come by the grace of our God and of our Lord Jesus Christ.*

> *(2 Thessalonians 1:11-12,* PARAPHRASED*)*

Paul's prayer is that in the midst of persecution and tribulation, we would be conquerors—and more than conquerors—not waiting to be rescued at the brink of defeat. While the world around them grew darker by the day, he expected them to shine all the brighter to the point that the glory of God shone through them in all their deeds and accomplishments. Would God ask any less of us today?

RECOGNIZED AS—AND ENABLED TO BE— WORTHY OF HIS CALLING

While Paul finished his first epistle to the Thessalonians by praying for their sanctification, he begins his second epistle by praying they would be worthy of the calling they had in Christ. Paul knew they had been called to spread the Gospel throughout Macedonia. And knowing that they had set themselves apart for it and dedicated themselves to it, he now prayed that they would be up to the task.

It was not that their calling was special or unique—individual callings for believers during the first century are unlikely to be very different from our calling to spread the Gospel and expand the kingdom of God today. However, Paul did not want them to underestimate the spiritual strength they would need to accomplish these goals. To be counted "worthy" of this calling was to be recognized as capable of fulfilling it. Yet sin threatened their success as much as complacency. They were doing well, the Word was going forth, and it was coming rather easily. Would they now give in to the temptation to assume it would always come easily, that there was really no reason to press on to what God was calling them to do? In praying that they would be counted worthy, Paul is praying for their further sanctification and preparation for the task, especially as the task grew more difficult—and evermore to a deeper holiness.

What Christian concept could possibly be more difficult than that of spiritual holiness? It's an easy concept to understand—simply living a life that does not offend God, avoids sin, and is blameless before all, a life filled with spiritual strength and purity to do good. Easy to understand but difficult to do.

Some saw holiness as nothing more than another call to a system of dos and don'ts—a call to develop a new "law" to govern behavior. Others saw it as a call to live devoid of all physical pleasures. Others took the "set apart"-ness of the call for sanctification to the extreme and locked themselves away in remote places where they hoped to escape the sinful world. New groups of "Pharisees" and "Sadducees" appeared with "heavy burdens, hard to bear, and [laid] them on men's shoulders; but they themselves [would] not move them with one of their fingers" (Matthew 23:4 NKJV [insert added]).

The call to holiness seemed to be some type of call back to a form of living by laws—where freedom in the Spirit was again traded for legalism and false religion. Yet Paul's definition was different. He emphasized freedom in Christ—"all things are lawful" (1 Corinthians 6:12; 10:23)—but choosing what was best out of that for *growth toward Christ.* If there was a principle for the day that could be applied it was: "What will bring me closer to—and make me more like—Jesus?" As Paul wrote to the Corinthians:

> Do you not know that the wicked will not inherit the kingdom of God? Do not be deceived: Neither the sexually immoral nor idolaters nor adulterers nor male prostitutes nor homosexual offenders nor thieves nor the greedy nor drunkards nor slanderers nor swindlers will inherit the kingdom of God. And that is what some of you were. But you were washed, you were sanctified, you were justified in the name of the Lord

Jesus Christ and by the Spirit of our God. "Everything
is permissible for me"—*but not everything is beneficial.*
"Everything is permissible for me"—*but I will not be
mastered by anything.*

—*1 Corinthians 6:9-12* NIV (emphasis added)

And again later in the same letter:

All things are lawful, but not all things are profitable.
All things are lawful, *but not all things edify.* Let no
one seek his own good, but that of his neighbor.

—*1 Corinthians 10:23-24* NASB (emphasis added)

Avoid the weights and burdens that will keep you from finishing
your race in Christ:

Let us lay aside every weight, and *the sin which so
easily ensnares us,* and let us run with endurance the
race that is set before us, looking unto Jesus, the
author and finisher of our faith, who for the joy that
was set before Him endured the cross, despising the
shame, and has sat down at the right hand of the
throne of God.

—*Hebrews 12:1-2* NKJV (emphasis added)

An example of this might be how Jesus healed. He didn't allow
himself to be weighed down with certain methods. Instead, He focused
on getting the job done. In one case, Jesus laid His hands on the blind
and commanded them to see; (See Matthew 9:27-30; 20:29-34.) in
another case he simply commanded the man's sight to return. (See
Mark 10:46-52.) One account has Jesus spitting on the ground,

making mud, and laying it on the person's eyes, (See John 9:1-7.) and in another he spit in the man's face! (See Mark 8:22-26.) All had the same problem—blindness—yet each, by the Spirit, received a different prescription for healing. It was not a case of Jesus' method as much as His sensitivity and obedience to the Spirit of God within Him. Jesus didn't just open a little book, turn to the section on "Healing the Blind," and follow the directions set forth there. Instead, He listened to the voice of the Spirit inside—a channel He kept open through constant communication with His Father—and obeyed what He was told to do. And, as a result, all of these people were healed.

Jesus—and for that matter, Paul as well—walked as renegades in the face of "religious" leaders not because of their lack of holiness, but because they walked by the dictates of the living, breathing Spirit of God rather than by a dusty and dead set of laws, rules, and regulations. As each person addressed is unique, God's response to each can also be unique, and for that, we must go directly to Him to know how to act rather than simply reference some code of behavior we have memorized in the past.

Now don't misunderstand. There are some actions and behaviors that are sin and should be avoided at all costs, but within acceptable behavior there is still always a range of possible responses. What the Spirit of God tells you to do will always line up with what the Word of God tells you is right. Yet the best behavior for a given situation will always be the one the Spirit of God shows you, even if it is unconventional—and it is in your obedience to what the Spirit of God shows you that true holiness and worthiness are found.

Thus how are you "enabled" to fulfill God's calling for your life on the earth? Through keeping in constant contact with headquarters in heaven and simply following God's instructions in all things.

FULFILLING THE GOOD PLEASURE
OF HIS GOODNESS

It is possible to get a job done by simply meeting the minimum requirements. But God has called us to do every job with excellence. That's what Paul meant by praying that we would "fulfill the good pleasure of His goodness." When we do, we almost always come out feeling stronger and happier.

"Fulfilling the good pleasure of His goodness" and "fulfilling the work to which He has called you with power" is thus not simply getting the job done, but it is finishing the race more "whole" than we began it, and that every life touched along the way would also be more "whole" for having been part of that success.

EXPERIENCING THE GLORY OF GOD

The most common ending to all of Paul's prayers is that what we become, what we do, and how we live our lives would all work together to bring glory to God the Father. Yet at the end of this prayer, he adds to it a slightly different nuance—not only that God would be glorified through us, but *that we would experience His glory as well.*

In the movie *Chariots of Fire,* about missionary and Olympic gold medalist Eric Liddel, he says, "I believe that God made me for a purpose—for China. But He also made me fast. And when I run, I feel His pleasure. To give it up would be to hold Him in contempt....To win is to honor Him." In the natural, it would seem there is little glory at a sporting event outside of winning. But Eric Liddel understood two types of glory: the glory of becoming an Olympic gold medalist and the glory of giving his life for God. He felt God's pleasure as he did his best to win for himself and for the glory of God—his victory becoming a testimony to God's greatness.

God has called us to similar success in the field or occupation in which He has gifted us. That should not be at the expense of all else that He has called us to in life, including walking in integrity, fulfilling the Great Commission, committing to a full and satisfying family life. God wants us to live excellently and find success as a testimony to others of His greatness, but success at the expense of any of the other areas of His promises is no testimony at all. It is our job to pursue His will and live for His pleasure.

SPIRITUAL VICTORIES

We can't expect to win spiritual victories unless we are commited to spending time in spiritual training. If we don't show discipline in choosing the things that will bring us closer to God over the things that will draw us away from Him, how can we expect to inherit true spiritual riches?

Paul's prayer here for the Thessalonians is for full—whole—victory as they work toward the crown God has for them in Christ Jesus. He wants them to accomplish their mission to spread the Gospel and God's kingdom, and do it in a way that allows them to fully enjoy their relationship with Him, their families, their personal lives, their reputations, their careers, their physical health, their mental and emotional health, and their prosperity.

As you meditate upon, study, and pray this prayer for yourself and others, may you plug into this fullness and experience His glory more and more in all you do! God is calling you to great things—enjoy every step along the way to accomplishing them in His full pleasure.

PRAYING 2 THESSALONIANS 1:11-12 FOR YOURSELF

Father,

In the name of Jesus, I praise and thank You for the faith and love You have put into me and what it is doing to transform my world into Your kingdom on earth. I thank You also for the promise that Your Son will come again soon, and that our victory over the devil and his followers will be manifested.

Because of these promises and gifts, I pray that I would be counted worthy—and able to accomplish—the calling Your life has given me on the earth. May my accomplishment of that calling and purpose be to Your full pleasure; I pray that I would leave no area of life unfilled in its accomplishment, and that all I touch would come to greater wholeness by coming in contact with me.

Lord, help me to achieve all the things I have set my faith to accomplish—the things You have called me to do and the good I have seen that needs to be done—through Your power and to Your glory. I pray that Your glory would encompass me on this earth as I experience Your presence and pleasure as a testimony that I am living the way You have called me to live.

Now let all of these things happen according to Your grace and that of Your Son, my Lord and Savior, Jesus Christ.

Amen.

PRAYING 2 THESSALONIANS 1:11-12 FOR OTHERS

Father,

In the name of Jesus, I praise and thank You for the faith and love active in the life of _____ and what it is doing to bring Your kingdom to this earth. I thank You also for the promise that Your Son will come again soon, and that our victory on the earth over the devil and his followers is assured. Because of these promises and gifts, I pray that _____ would be counted worthy—and able to accomplish—the calling You have given _____ on the earth. May _____'s accomplishment of that calling and purpose be to Your full pleasure; I pray that no part of _____ life would be unfulfilled and that all whom _____ touches in _____ walk with You would come to greater wholeness.

Lord, help _____ accomplish all the things _____ has set _____ faith to accomplish—the things You have called _____ to do and the good that _____ has seen that needs to be done—through Your power and to your glory. I pray that Your glory would encompass _____ on this earth as _____ experiences Your presence and pleasure as evidence that _____ is living the way You have called _____ to live.

Now let all of these things happen according to Your grace and that of Your Son, my Lord and Savior, Jesus Christ.

Amen.

PAUL'S PRAYER IN CONTEXT THROUGH VARIOUS TRANSLATIONS

2 Thessalonians 1:3-12 from the *New King James Version* (NKJV)

We are bound to thank God always for you, brethren, as it is fitting, because your faith grows exceedingly, and the love of every one of you all abounds toward each other, so that we ourselves boast of you among the churches of God for your patience and faith in all your persecutions and tribulations that you endure, which is manifest evidence of the righteous judgment of God, that you may be counted worthy of the kingdom of God, for which you also suffer; since it is a righteous thing with God to repay with tribulation those who trouble you, and to give you who are troubled rest with us when the Lord Jesus is revealed from heaven with His mighty angels, in flaming fire taking vengeance on those who do not know God, and on those who do not obey the gospel of our Lord Jesus Christ. These shall be punished with everlasting destruction from the presence of the Lord and from the glory of His power, when He comes, in that Day, to be glorified in His saints and to be admired among all those who believe, because our testimony among you was believed.

Therefore we also pray always for you that our God would count you worthy of this calling, and fulfill all the good pleasure of His goodness and the work of faith with power, that the name of our Lord Jesus Christ may be glorified in you, and you in Him, according to the grace of our God and the Lord Jesus Christ.

2 Thessalonians 1:3-12 from the *New Century Version* (NCV)

We must always thank God for you, brothers and sisters. This is only right, because your faith is growing more and more, and the love that every one of you has for each other is increasing. So we brag about you to the other churches of God. We tell them about the way you continue to be strong and have faith even though you are being treated badly and are suffering many troubles.

This is proof that God is right in his judgment. He wants you to be counted worthy of his kingdom for which you are suffering. God will do what is right. He will give trouble to those who trouble you. And he will give rest to you who are troubled and to us also when the Lord Jesus appears with burning fire from heaven with his powerful angels. Then he will punish those who do not know God and who do not obey the Good News about our Lord Jesus Christ. Those people will be punished with a destruction that continues forever. They will be kept away from the Lord and from his great power. This will happen on the day when the Lord Jesus comes to receive glory because of his holy people. And all the people who have believed will be amazed at Jesus. You will be in that group, because you believed what we told you.

That is why we always pray for you, asking our God to help you live the kind of life he called you to live. We pray that with his power God will help you do the good things you want and perform the works that come from your faith. We pray all this so that the name of our Lord Jesus Christ will have glory in you, and you will have glory in him. That glory comes from the grace of our God and the Lord Jesus Christ.

2 Thessalonians 1:3-12 from the *Good News Translation* (GNT)

Our brothers, we must thank God at all times for you. It is right for us to do so, because your faith is growing so much and the love each of you has for the others is becoming greater. That is why we ourselves boast about you in the churches of God. We boast about the way you continue to endure and believe through all the persecutions and sufferings you are experiencing.

All of this proves that God's judgment is just and as a result you will become worthy of his Kingdom, for which you are suffering. God will do what is right: he will bring suffering on those who make you suffer, and he will give relief to you who suffer and to us as well. He will do this when the Lord Jesus appears from heaven with his mighty angels, with a flaming fire, to punish those who reject God and who do not obey the Good News about our Lord Jesus. They will suffer the punishment of eternal destruction, separated from the presence of the Lord and from his glorious might, when he comes on that Day to receive glory from all his people and honor from all who believe. You too will be among them, because you have believed the message that we told you.

That is why we always pray for you. We ask our God to make you worthy of the life he has called you to live. May he fulfill by his power all your desire for goodness and complete your work of faith. In this way the name of our Lord Jesus will receive glory from you, and you from him, by the grace of our God and of the Lord Jesus Christ.

chapter ten

ESTABLISH ME IN YOUR TRUTH

Our Lord Jesus Christ himself, and God, even our Father,
which hath loved us, and hath given us everlasting
consolation and good hope through grace, comfort your
hearts, and stablish you in every good word and work.

2 Thessalonians 2:16-17

What does deception do to a person?

Nestled against the Front Range of the Rocky Mountains in Boulder, Colorado, the U.S. government maintains offices for the National Institute of Standards and Technologies (NIST), the mission of which is "to develop and promote measurement, standards, and technology to enhance productivity, facilitate trade, and improve the quality of life." It is here that an atomic clock is maintained that sends out the correct time via satellite all over the world. It is also here that the Weights and Measures Division uses the latest technologies available to ensure that all of our measurements—lengths, weights, and volumes—are as accurate as possible. Over half of the U.S. Gross Domestic Product is affected by the measures established by NIST.

The Bible tells us:

> A false balance is an abomination to the LORD,
> but a just weight is His delight.
>
> —*Proverbs 11:1* NASB

The marketplace in Solomon's day was filled with dishonesty. Merchants manipulated the weights in order to squeeze as much money as possible from each purchase. Over time, the merchant would increase his profits by 10 percent because of his false weights—a very subtle form of theft that was difficult to prove.

Nowadays, such deception is rare because of the efforts of organizations such as NIST that go to great effort and expense to make sure our measurements are "true." They check and recheck their calculations to keep them as true as modern technology can make them.

We would be well advised to be just as diligent to ensure that the "truths" we build our lives upon are also as precisely "true." In matters of truth, we cannot be complacent and assume that everything we hear is true. We must carefully check things out ourselves by the plumb lines of God's Word and the witness of the Holy Spirit in our hearts.

Because of this, Paul emphasizes that it is those who "love the truth" who make their callings and elections sure. It is also what he prays for them in 2 Thessalonians 2:17 when he requests that they be "established in every good word and work" (NKJV). He was praying that they would fully know the truth, apply that truth, be firmly founded in that truth, and as a result that truth would set them free in all areas of their lives, just as Jesus said it would:

> [Jesus said,] "If you abide in My word, you are My disciples indeed. And you shall know the truth, and the truth shall make you free."
>
> —*John 8:31-32* NKJV

By abiding in His words—meditating upon them diligently and living them out in your life—you will know the truth, and that truth can indeed set you free from all that could hold you back from accomplishing God's purpose and calling for your life. The truth can keep you correctly on course to all that God promised and called you to walk out on the earth.

Shortly after Paul had written his first epistle to the Thessalonians, he heard that false teachers had gone to Thessalonica carrying a false epistle with his name on it. So in his second letter to them, after correcting the false teaching, he prayed for their establishment—that they would be firmly founded in the truth he had first taught them: *May our Lord and Savior Jesus Christ Himself and God our Father—who loved us and by His grace (His unmerited favor towards us) has already given us eternal comfort (everlasting consolation) and good (firm, well-founded) hope to:*

(a) *Comfort and encourage your hearts (your inner persons).*

(b) *Encourage and establish you [make you steadfast and unswerving] in every good word (truth).*

(c) *Encourage and establish you [make you steadfast and unswerving] in every good work (good deed and action).*

—*(2 Thessalonians 2:16-17,* PARAPHRASED*)*

Paul was praying that they would hold on to the truth he had taught them and use it as the foundation for all they were doing. With the truth well established in their hearts and minds, he hoped they would be impervious to false teaching.

In our time of diverse teachings, countless sects, denominations, and cults, and satellite television where anyone with a message and the right amount of money can find a place to teach the naïve and uninformed, we need more than ever to cling to the truths God has set forth in His

Word and by His Spirit. More than ever, we need to learn to recognize and be established in God's truth if we are going to escape deception.

LOVING THE TRUTH

In his absence and after Timothy's first report back on the events happening in Macedonia (to which Paul had responded in his first letter to the Thessalonians), someone had taken a false letter to them stating that the Rapture had already happened! The bogus document declared that Nero was the antichrist, Jesus had already returned, and they were living in the midst of the tribulation. What a stir this must have caused! What would such news do to their evangelistic outreaches? What would they tell the churches they had planted?

So it is that Paul, seemingly on the heels of his first letter to them, writes another letter to set the record straight. He writes that this other letter was, in fact, a forgery and that none of these things had yet occurred. Then he carefully reminded them that they had covered the order of end-time events when they had first been together. He patiently went over the things that would occur before Christ's return and cautioned them not to be fooled by false reports. Paul reminded them of the great apostasy that would come first and draw many away into deception. And once again, he comforted them, restating that the only ones who would be deceived would be those who "did not receive the love of the truth, that they might be saved" (2 Thessalonians 2:10 NKJV). Paul goes on to say:

> We should always give thanks to God for you,
> brethren beloved by the Lord, because God has chosen

you from the beginning for salvation *through sanctifi-cation by the Spirit and faith in the truth.*

—*2 Thessalonians 2:13* NASB (emphasis added)

How are we to be saved from deception? Through "sanctification by the Spirit" and "faith [which works by love] in the truth." The Word of God and the Spirit of God are our best tests of the truth—but we must continue to seek the truth at all times with the same love that makes us pursue knowing Christ better each day.

When we first meet Jesus, recognize Him as the Truth, and make Him our Lord and Savior, we are saved. We have stepped through the gate—out of Satan's jurisdiction and into God's kingdom. After that, it's each person's choice. The further we walk into the truth, the further we travel into God's kingdom. We can stand just inside the threshold, or we can keep walking until the kingdom surrounds us and becomes part of us.

As we move forward, we will see new aspects of truth, like the features of a mountain we climb or a forest we hike through. We will encounter the smell of it; we will be able to touch and taste its fruit. We will not only learn our own way around better, but soon we will be guiding others.

Only those who truly love truth and are willing to pursue it to the point that it changes them will ever experience the fullness of God's kingdom. Those who accept whatever they are told will build their lives on partial truths and their faith will waver because of it. They will be living their lives with weights and measures that are just a little bit off. In the end, they will be saved, but they will never really fulfill the purpose for which they were called.

So what does deception do? It weakens the structural integrity of anything we want to construct for God, including lives that give glory to Him. It also pushes us off course and keeps us from fulfilling our God-given purpose. This is why Paul prayed that his spiritual children would be established in the truth.

THE GOD OF CONSOLATION, COMFORT, AND HOPE

Being corrected is never easy. Some people prefer to cling to lies rather than admit they've invested in deception. The greater the lie they have believed, the more difficult it is to discard it and turn again to the truth. That's why "loving the truth" is so important. Being constantly in pursuit of it and making small adjustments to make sure your weights and measures are dead on is the only way to ensure the integrity of your faith.

Paul could have called for judgment when he realized that the Thessalonians had fallen for a false doctrine. Instead, he appealed to "God the Father, who has loved us, and through His grace given us everlasting consolation and good hope" to "comfort your hearts and establish you in every good word and work." Paul is requesting that they be restored in a spirit of love and reconciliation.

This is a wonderful lesson for those who realize they have fallen for deception. Paul's prayer reaches across the bands of eternity to comfort and console them, just as it did for the Thessalonians. They, too, can know that the Spirit of truth is within them, not to condemn them, but to establish their righteousness. (See John 16:7-15.)

Paul's prayer asks that the Thessalonians would receive hope—but not just hope, "good hope." Good hope is beneficial hope. It's hope that sets us back on the path and gives us the promise of future possibilities.

THE GREATEST ADVENTURE OF ALL— LIVING FOR JESUS

All great adventures include obstacles, hardships, and mistakes. Should our adventure of following Christ be any different? Satan won't waste time troubling those who are not troubling him—he is fighting a tough enough battle without wasting his time on ineffective believers.

The truth of the matter was that the Thessalonians were doing great things. Because of them the Gospel was spreading throughout Macedonia and Achaia. Those false messengers were sent to cripple their testimonies and destroy their confidence. Paul sent them correction not to belittle them for falling for the deception; he was interested in reestablishing them in the truth so that they could get back to doing the great things they had been involved in before. He wanted to restore their boldness and rekindle their hope in God's calling. He wanted to make them stronger so that they would be less vulnerable in the future.

It is interesting to note that Jesus likened both the false doctrines of the Pharisees and Sadducees (see Matthew 16:6-12). and the true doctrine of the kingdom of God (see Matthew 13:33). to yeast leavening bread—just a little bit of either will affect the entire lump. Are you an advocate for truth?

Meditate on the truth of God's Word and pray that you would be more and more firmly founded in it. Pray the same for those in your church, your church's leadership, and in your family and community.

Remember that "Unless the LORD builds the house, they labor in vain who build it" (Psalm 127:1 NKJV). Continually test the trueness of your measurements against His so that all you build and accomplish in your life will be according to His exact standards of truth and will stand the test of eternity.

PRAYING 2 THESSALONIANS 2:16-17 FOR YOURSELF

Father,

In the name of Jesus, I pray that You—the Father of our Lord Jesus Christ, who first loved me and by Your grace has given me everlasting comfort and consolation through the indwelling of Your Holy Spirit—would infuse me with Your truth and give me a good, effective, and solid hope in what You have promised me in Your Word and what You have called me individually to accomplish during my time on the earth. I pray that You would comfort my heart with Your grace and presence, and establish and firmly found me in every good word of Your truth so that I understand every aspect of it, can base my life upon it, and communicate it to others.

Lord, establish and firmly found me in every good action or work of Your truth so that I may walk in every aspect of it and effectively reach out to others in all that I do.

Amen.

PRAYING 2 THESSALONIANS 2:16-17
FOR OTHERS

Father,

In the name of Jesus, I pray that You—the Father of our Lord Jesus Christ, who first loved us and by Your grace has given us everlasting comfort and consolation through the indwelling of Your Holy Spirit—would infuse _____ with Your truth and give _____ a good, effective, and solid hope in what You have promised _____ in Your Word and what You would have each of us, both individually and corporately, accomplish during our time on the earth. I pray that You would comfort _____'s heart with Your grace and presence, and establish and firmly found _____ in every good word of Your truth so that _____ understands every aspect of it, can base _____ life upon it, and communicate it to others.

Lord, establish and firmly found _____ in every good action or work of Your truth so that _____ can walk in every aspect of it and effectively reach out to others in all that _____ does.

Amen.

PAUL'S PRAYER IN CONTEXT THROUGH
VARIOUS TRANSLATIONS

2 Thessalonians 2:13-17 from the
International Standard Version (ISV)

At all times we are obligated to thank God for you, brothers who are loved by the Lord, because God chose you to be the first fruits for salvation through sanctification by the Spirit and through faith in the truth. With this purpose in mind, he called you through our proclamation of the gospel so that you would obtain the glory of our Lord Jesus Christ. So then, brothers, stand firm, and cling to the traditions that you were taught by us, either by word of mouth or by our letter.

May our Lord Jesus Christ himself and God our Father, who loved us and by his grace gave us eternal comfort and good hope, encourage your hearts and strengthen you in every good work and word.

2 Thessalonians 2:13-17 form the *Good News Translation* (GNT)

We must thank God at all times for you, brothers, you whom the Lord loves. For God chose you as the first to be saved by the Spirit's power to make you his holy people and by your faith in the truth. God called you to this through the Good News we preached to you; he called you to possess your share of the glory of our Lord Jesus Christ. So then, our brothers, stand firm and hold on to those truths which we taught you, both in our preaching and in our letter.

May our Lord Jesus Christ himself and God our Father, who loved us and in his grace gave us unfailing courage and a firm hope, encourage you and strengthen you to always do and say what is good.

2 Thessalonians 2:13-17 from the *Contemporary English Version* (CEV)

My friends, the Lord loves you, and it is only natural for us to thank God for you. God chose you to be the first ones to be saved. His Spirit made you holy, and you put your faith in the truth. God used our preaching as his way of inviting you to share in the glory of our Lord Jesus Christ. My friends, that's why you must remain faithful and follow closely what we taught you in person and by our letters.

God our Father loves us. He is kind and has given us eternal comfort and a wonderful hope. We pray that our Lord Jesus Christ and God our Father will encourage you and help you always to do and say the right thing.

2 Thessalonians 2:13-17 from the *Amplified Bible* (AMP)

But we, brethren beloved by the Lord, ought and are obligated [as those who are in debt] to give thanks always to God for you, because God chose you from the beginning as His first-fruits (first converts) for salvation through the sanctifying work of the [Holy] Spirit and [your] belief in (adherence to, trust in, and reliance on) the Truth.

[It was] to this end that He called you through our Gospel, so that you may obtain and share in the glory of our Lord Jesus Christ (the Messiah).

So then, brethren, stand firm and hold fast to the traditions and instructions which you were taught by us, whether by our word of mouth or by letter.

Now may our Lord Jesus Christ Himself and God our Father, Who loved us and gave us everlasting consolation and encouragement and well-founded hope through [His] grace (unmerited favor),

Comfort and encourage your hearts and strengthen them [make them steadfast and keep them unswerving] in every good work and word.

chapter eleven

INCREASE YOUR PATIENCE IN ME

The Lord direct your hearts into the love of God,
and into the patient waiting for Christ.
2 Thessalonians 3:5

The trouble with growing mature, building something worthwhile,
or inheriting the promises of God is that it takes *so long.* In our world
of microwave popcorn, On-Demand television, guaranteed 20-minute-
or-less pizza deliveries, and one-day Las Vegas no-fault divorces, our
culture does not encourage the art of waiting. However, a tree takes
years if not decades to come into fullness—and, in Psalm 1, it is the
tree, not the microwave popcorn, to which God compares us:

> Blessed is the man
> Who walks not in the counsel of the ungodly,
> Nor stands in the path of sinners,
> Nor sits in the seat of the scornful;
> But his delight is in the law of the LORD,
> And in His law he meditates day and night.
> *He shall be like a tree*
> *Planted by the rivers of water,*
> *That brings forth its fruit in its season,*
> *Whose leaf also shall not wither;*
> *And whatever he does shall prosper.*
> —*Psalm 1:1-3* NKJV (emphasis added)

Paul must have been seeing this with regard to the believers in Thessalonica as well. Their quick success was having repercussions—persecutions, trials, and false teachings. They were learning that the Christian life is more than a 100-meter dash; it was now time to set in for the marathon.

To this end, Paul prayed for them: *May your active pursuit of our Lord and Savior Jesus Christ:*

(a) *Lead you more and more into the fullness of God's love.*

(b) *Lead you into patience, endurance, long-suffering, and steadfastness of Christ himself as you await His return.*

—(2 Thessalonians 3:5, PARAPHRASED)

Paul wanted to ensure that they would survive the difficult times ahead. More than that, he longed to see them energetically thrive through it all for that joy on the other side. (See Galatians 6:9.)

LOVE IS PATIENT

Before Paul asks that they have patience, he asks that they have love, because without love, patient endurance is only a smoldering, internalization of anger that will someday explode into something else. It is the love of God that gives patience its power to change unrighteous circumstances. Without the sense that we are enduring for the blessing of those persecuting us, patience can be little more than putting up with suffering.

The first, and strongest, attribute of the God kind of love that Paul lists in his most famous discourse on the subject in 1 Corinthians 13 is love's patience.

> Love is patient…is not provoked, does not take into
> account a wrong suffered…bears all things, believes
> all things, hopes all things, endures all things. Love
> never fails.
>
> —*1 Corinthians 13:4, 5, 7-8* NASB

According to this, there is nothing in God's love that needs to strike back. It is patient. It endures long. It is not provoked. It keeps no list of offenses against it to use as evidence of wrongdoing at a later date. It always believes the best of others, never loses hope, bears all, endures all, and never fails.

Pastor Richard Wurmbrand spent fourteen years in prison in Romania under a Communist regime on account of his faith. He was repeatedly tortured and wore the scars of those tortures over his entire body. For a good portion of his imprisonment, Wurmbrand's family thought he was dead because that is what Romanian officials had told them. Many of the things done to him to make him renounce Christ are virtually unspeakable. And yet, when he was finally ransomed by believers in the West and set free, one of the first things he did was start a ministry called "Jesus to the Communist World," which is known today as "The Voice of the Martyrs." In his best-selling book about his experiences, entitled *Tortured for Christ,* Pastor Wurmbrand wrote:

> A flower, if you bruise it under your feet, rewards you
> by giving you its perfume. Likewise Christians, tortured
> by the Communists, rewarded their torturers with love.
> We brought many of our jailors to Christ. And we are
> dominated by one desire: to give Communists who
> have made us suffer the best we have, the salvation
> which comes from our Lord Jesus Christ.[7]

If we cannot love with such love those who persecute us, how do we expect God to step in and defend us? As he said again in 1 Corinthians 13, such endurance without suffering is meaningless:

> If I surrender my body to be burned, but do not have love, it profits me nothing.
>
> —*1 Corinthians 13:3* NASB

HOPE, FAITH, AND PATIENCE

For us to endure, however, we must have a picture—"a confident favorable expectation"—of what is ahead for us. Again, our example in this is Jesus himself:

> Wherefore seeing we also are compassed about with so great a cloud of witnesses, let us lay aside every weight, and the sin which doth so easily beset us, and let us run with patience the race that is set before us, Looking unto Jesus the author and finisher of our faith; *who for the joy that was set before him endured the cross, despising the shame, and is set down at the right hand of the throne of God.*
>
> —*Hebrews 12:1-2* (emphasis added)

Jesus was able to endure the hardships of the Cross because He had looked beyond them to the joy on the other side. He had settled it in His prayer in the Garden of Gethsemane when He prayed, "Not my will, but thine, be done" (Luke 22:42). He would not give in to the temptation to give up, call twelve legions of angels, and be delivered from that degrading death. All this He did for the joy that lay on the other side of the Cross—our salvation.

In the book of Romans, Paul echoes this sentiment:

> If we hope for that we see not, then do we with
> patience wait for it.
>
> —*Romans 8:25*

We do not see with our natural eyes—hope sees with spiritual eyes. Our spiritual eyes see what God has ahead for us—then we can, with patient endurance, wait for it.

Sometimes, that hope is little more than knowing that there is something more in God if we just keep pushing on and following His voice. But even when it is not yet clearly defined, we must exercise our faith and set out to do what God is calling us to do. We must persevere in order to claim the prize that lies on the other side of our suffering. Whether we have one step or a hundred, we must trust God. For as the Scriptures say:

> God is fair; he will not forget the work you did and
> the love you showed for him by helping his people.
> And he will remember that you are still helping them.
> We want each of you to go on with the same hard
> work all your lives so you will surely get what you
> hope for. We do not want you to become lazy. *Be like
> those who through faith and patience will receive what
> God has promised.*
>
> —*Hebrews 6:10-12* NCV (emphasis added)

Though we may not always be able to see it with our natural eyes, we can be assured that God is working out the things He has promised. As Solomon said:

> As thou knowest not what is the way of the spirit, nor how the bones do grow in the womb of her that is with child: even so thou knowest not the works of God who maketh all.
>
> —*Ecclesiastes 11:5*

Just as a baby grows in the womb of its mother, hidden away from our natural sight, God's promises take shape in the womb of God's wisdom, growing and maturing until they burst forth into our lives fully formed.

Keep doing your part, keep obeying, and God will take care of His part. In His perfect timing, your dream, your purpose, your calling *will be born,* just as God promised!

Paul saw such patience and endurance in the Thessalonians:

> We give thanks to God always for you all, making mention of you in our prayers; remembering without ceasing your work of faith, and labour of love, and *patience of hope in our Lord Jesus Christ,* in the sight of God and our Father; knowing, brethren beloved, your election of God.
>
> —*1 Thessalonians 1:2-4* (emphasis added)

> We ourselves glory in you in the churches of God *for your patience and faith in all your persecutions and tribulations that ye endure.*
>
> —*2 Thessalonians 1:4* (emphasis added)

Yet he still prayed that they would stay faithful in the love of God. And his prayer is for your life as well. Stay faithful. Persevere until you have accomplished all that God has called you to do.

PAUL TAUGHT PATIENCE BY EXAMPLE

Paul lived the truth he was teaching the Thessalonians. The prayer he prayed for them was one he prayed for his own life. Second Corinthians 11 tells of the things he patiently endured:

> I am more: in labors more abundant, in stripes above measure, in prisons more frequently, in deaths often. From the Jews five times I received forty stripes minus one. Three times I was beaten with rods; once I was stoned; three times I was shipwrecked; a night and a day I have been in the deep; in journeys often, in perils of waters, in perils of robbers, in perils of my own countrymen, in perils of the Gentiles, in perils in the city, in perils in the wilderness, in perils in the sea, in perils among false brethren; in weariness and toil, in sleeplessness often, in hunger and thirst, in fastings often, in cold and nakedness—besides the other things, what comes upon me daily: my deep concern for all the churches.
>
> —*2 Corinthians 11:23-28* NKJV

Paul's testimony is that although these things hindered him and prevented his success, in the end he had "fought the good fight...finished the race, [and]...kept the faith" (2 Timothy 4:7 NKJV [insert added]). He faced much greater obstacles than the vast majority of us will ever know, and yet *he prevailed*. In the final letter we have from him in the Bible, he called Timothy to follow the same path of patient endurance:

> You followed my teaching, conduct, purpose, faith, *patience*, love, *perseverance*, persecutions, and sufferings, such as happened to me at Antioch, at Iconium and at Lystra; *what persecutions I endured, and out of them all the Lord rescued me!*
>
> —*2 Timothy 3:10-11* NASB (emphasis added)

Which persecutions did God rescue him from? Those that he *endured*. In other words, it was not the hardship that could defeat him; it was only his own quitting in the midst of that hardship that could have done that. God would see him through anything He had called Paul to do, if only Paul stayed on God's true course *through* it to the other side.

For those following God's lordship of their lives today, the challenge is no different, even if the persecutions and trials are. We must push through to what God is calling us to with the same patient endurance required of a spiritual triathlon or marathon participant. We are in it for the long haul. If we fall, we must get up and keep running. If we take a wrong turn along the way, we must retrace our steps until we are back on the right path. As long as we head toward God's calling for our lives and listen carefully to the instruction and direction of our coach, we cannot lose. And just as Paul, we must apply ourselves to the acquisition of that calling:

> Do you not know that those who run in a race all run, but one receives the prize? Run in such a way

that you may obtain it. And everyone who competes
for the prize is temperate in all things. Now they do it
to obtain a perishable crown, but we for an imperish-
able crown. Therefore I run thus: not with uncertainty. Thus I fight: not as one who beats the air. But
I discipline my body and bring it into subjection, lest,
when I have preached to others, I myself should
become disqualified.

—*1 Corinthians 9:24-27* NKJV

If you run your race with the same certainty and the same patient
endurance as Paul did, you will one day wear the crown God has set
aside for you in heaven.

PRAYING 2 THESSALONIANS 3:5
FOR YOURSELF

Father,

*In the name of Jesus, I praise and thank You for being the God of
love, the God of hope, and the God of peace. Because of these, I
pray that You would direct my heart into, and strengthen my
inner person with, Your eternal love, so that I might, with the
patience of Christ, endure the race You have set before me and
stick to it faithfully until the day of Christ.*

Amen.

PRAYING 2 THESSALONIANS 3:5 FOR OTHERS

Father,

In the name of Jesus, I praise and thank You for being the God of love, the God of hope, and the God of peace. Because of these, I pray that You would direct _____'s heart into, and strengthen _____ inner person with, Your eternal love, so that _____ might, with the patience of Christ, endure the race You have set before _____ and stick faithfully to it until the day of Christ.

Amen.

PAUL'S PRAYER IN CONTEXT THROUGH VARIOUS TRANSLATIONS

2 Thessalonians 3:3-5 from the *New American Standard Bible* (NASB)

The Lord is faithful, and He will strengthen and protect you from the evil one.

We have confidence in the Lord concerning you, that you are doing and will continue to do what we command.

May the Lord direct your hearts into the love of God and into the steadfastness of Christ.

2 Thessalonians 3:3-5 from the *New International Version* (NIV)

The Lord is faithful, and he will strengthen and protect you from the evil one. We have confidence in the Lord that you are doing and will continue to do the things we command. May the Lord direct your hearts into God's love and Christ's perseverance.

2 Thessalonians 3:3-5 from the *New Century Version* (NCV)

The Lord is faithful and will give you strength and will protect you from the Evil One. The Lord makes us feel sure that you are doing and will continue to do the things we told you. May the Lord lead your hearts into God's love and Christ's patience.

2 Thessalonians 3:3-5 from *the Message* (THE MESSAGE)

The Master never lets us down. He'll stick by you and protect you from evil.

Because of the Master, we have great confidence in you. We know you're doing everything we told you and will continue doing it. May the Master take you by the hand and lead you along the path of God's love and Christ's endurance.

**2 Thessalonians 3:3-5 from the
Contemporary English Version (CEV)**

The Lord can be trusted to make you strong and protect you from harm. He has made us sure that you are obeying what we taught you and that you will keep on obeying. I pray that the Lord will guide you to be as loving as God and as patient as Christ.

chapter twelve

GIVE US YOUR PEACE

The Lord of peace himself give you peace always
by all means. The Lord be with you all.
2 Thessalonians 3:16

In Paul's writings, he refers to God the Father with six different titles:

1. God of patience and consolation

2. God of hope

3. God of all comfort

4. God of our Lord Jesus Christ

5. God of love

6. God of peace

Of these, he refers to only one more than once—"the God of peace," which he uses five times. Here in 2 Thessalonians 3:16, Paul attributes this same quality to our Lord Jesus Christ. Paul must have realized the role "peace" plays in our understanding of the nature of God and Christ's victory on the Cross.

This prayer is a simple and straightforward one: *May the Lord of peace himself, our Lord and Savior Jesus Christ:*

(a) *Continually grant you His peace (the peace of living in His kingdom and will) in all situations and in every circumstance no matter what you face.*

(b) Be with you always (may you feel His presence at all times).
—(2 Thessalonians 3:16, PARAPHRASED*)*

Paul knew the Thessalonians had been bombarded and assailed with persecutions, trials, and false teachings. Their commendable work on behalf on the Gospel had made them targets. They needed peace—the peace that goes beyond understanding and adverse circumstances. After all, Jesus Christ had purchased that God-peace for them on the Cross. It was their birthright.

The Thessalonians learned that God's peace dwells in the presence of the risen Christ—the Prince of Peace—and that's where you can find it today.

PEACE FROM THE PRINCE OF PEACE

Of all of Paul's prayers, this is the only one that asks that our Lord and Savior grant it rather than God the Father, though he echoes this prayer to the Father in Romans by asking:

The God of peace be with you all. Amen.

—Romans 15:33

While it is God the Father who is the God of peace, it is Jesus who is the Lord and Prince of Peace. Jesus is the covenant partner through whom we have reconciliation with the Father. When He died on the Cross and rose again, Jesus reestablished our connection to God and the peace of God began to flow to us again.

Being justified by faith, we have peace with God
through our Lord Jesus Christ.

—Romans 5:1

And again:

> It pleased the Father that in Him all the fullness should
> dwell, and by Him to reconcile all things to Himself,
> by Him, whether things on earth or things in heaven,
> *having made peace through the blood of His cross.*
> —*Colossians 1:19-20* NKJV (emphasis added)

Today we often think of peace as being the absence of conflict
between individuals or nations, or the feeling of serenity we might have
in a quiet moment. Yet in Hebrew, the word peace—*shalom*—has a
much deeper and richer meaning. The word *shalom* means literally
"completeness, soundness, welfare, peace … safety, soundness (in body)
… health, prosperity … quiet, tranquility, contentment … friendship
of human relationships [and] with God especially in covenant relationship."[8] *Shalom* is one of the key words that describes our new covenant
relationship to God through Christ's blood and sacrifice, and it is the
term through which, when we enter back into covenant with God
through Christ, we become His *friend.*

God's definition of friendship goes way beyond our understanding of
the word today. The Old Testament uses it as a covenant term indicating the establishment of a bond sealed through the shedding of blood.
It literally includes the pledging of one's all to the protection, success,
health, and overall welfare of the other. It is, in essence, saying you will
do everything within your power to secure the *shalom* of the other. If
there is a need in the fields or concerning a business matter, you will be
there to help. If an enemy attacks, your sword will fight alongside that
of your friend's. If there is sickness, your resources are pledged to help
bring healing. And if there is death, your friend's family is as your own
family and will never go wanting as long as you can help it.

It is in this same spirit of covenant friendship that David welcomed Mephibosheth to his table in 2 Samuel 9. Because Mephibosheth was Jonathan's son, and David and Jonathan had been in covenant friendship with one another, David restored to Mephibosheth all of the lands of his father and grandfather, Saul, even though Saul hated David and had tried to kill him many times. David also made Mephibosheth a permanent guest at his table in the palace. David set out to ensure the *shalom* of Mephibosheth.

It is this kind of peace that Paul asks God to grant the Thessalonians—a full peace that rests in the confidence that God's resources are available to you no matter what you might face in the future. In a sense, Paul was praying that they would live "under the shadow of the Almighty" (Psalm 91:1).

How are we to live in this peace? By going to the foot of the Cross to receive Christ's redemptive sacrifice, and then by living continually in His presence through the work of the Holy Spirit. As Paul said again in Romans:

> [God] condemned sin in the flesh, that the righteous requirement of the law might be fulfilled in us who do not walk according to the flesh but according to the Spirit. For those who live according to the flesh set their minds on the things of the flesh, but those who live according to the Spirit, the things of the Spirit. For to be carnally minded is death, but *to be spiritually minded is life and peace.*
>
> —*Romans 8:3-6* NKJV (emphasis and insert added)

Another way of saying it is that our peace comes by our place in Christ:

In Christ Jesus you who once were far away have been brought near through the blood of Christ. *For he himself is our peace,* who has made the two one and has destroyed the barrier, the dividing wall of hostility, by abolishing in his flesh the law with its commandments and regulations. His purpose was to create in himself one new man out of the two, *thus making peace,* and in this one body to reconcile both of them to God through the cross, by which he put to death their hostility. *He came and preached peace to you who were far away and peace to those who were near* [both to the Gentiles and to the Jews].

—*Ephesians 2:13-17* NIV (emphasis and insert added)

Because Jesus is our peace, we have peace with God. No longer are we to be governed by the law with its commandments and regulations, but we are to live by the law of love and obedience to the Holy Spirit who now lives within us and guides us.

FOLLOW AFTER HIS PEACE

As we've discussed, the coming of the Holy Spirit to dwell in believers brought a new relationship between prayer and peace. Any anxiety or concern, any remembrance of someone, was a chance to pray and lay them before the Lord. As Paul wrote to the Philippians:

Be anxious for nothing, but in everything by prayer and supplication with thanksgiving let your requests be made known to God. *And the peace of God, which surpasses all comprehension, will guard your hearts and your minds in Christ Jesus.* Finally, brethren, whatever is true, whatever is honorable, whatever is right, whatever is pure, whatever is lovely, whatever is of good repute, if there is any excellence and if anything worthy of praise, dwell on these things. *The things you have learned and received and heard and seen in me, practice these things, and the God of peace will be with you.*

—*Philippians 4:6-9* NASB (emphasis added)

Here Paul speaks of a peace that is beyond comprehension—a peace that floods our hearts and minds as we lay our concerns before our Heavenly Father. When His peace comes, we can be sure what we prayed for has been answered. What a privilege!

We must be aware though that we must guard that peace from doubt and unbelief. Once we have our answer, we need to focus our minds on "whatever is true, whatever is honorable, whatever is right, whatever is pure, whatever is lovely, whatever is of good repute, if there is any excellence and if anything worthy of praise."

Peace can also be viewed as a weather vane directing us in the way we should be going. When we feel our peace slipping away, we must actively pursue it. In his last letter to Timothy, Paul told him to "pursue"—or as *The Message* version says, "run after"—peace and the other fruit of righteousness:

Run away from infantile indulgence. Run after mature righteousness—faith, love, *peace*—joining those who are in honest and serious prayer before God.

—*2 Timothy 2:22* THE MESSAGE (emphasis added)

Is the peace of God a constant in your life? If not, pursue it. Let it be the cornerstone of every decision, every relationship, every activity. In every aspect of your life, make it your constant conviction to "follow the peace." As Paul also instructed the Colossians:

> *The peace that Christ gives is to guide you in the decisions you make;* for it is to this peace that God has called you together in the one body.
>
> —*Colossians 3:15* GNT (emphasis added)

Why pursue peace? Because that is also where God's kingdom is:

> The kingdom of God is…righteousness and *peace* and joy in the Holy Spirit.
>
> —*Romans 14:17* NKJV (emphasis added)

THE GOSPEL OF PEACE

We are called to be ambassadors for Christ, ministers of reconciliation to God, and in these roles, we are to make "peace" part of our mission to the world. We are to share the gospel of peace with God with as many as we can. It is, in fact, part of our armor described in Ephesians 6: "your feet fitted with the readiness that comes from the gospel of peace" (Ephesians 6:15 NIV). Or as Paul again describes it in Romans, chapter 10:

> "Whoever calls on the name of the LORD shall be saved." How then shall they call on Him in whom they have not believed? And how shall they believe in Him of whom they have not heard? And how shall they hear without a preacher? And how shall they

preach unless they are sent? As it is written: "How beautiful are the feet of those who preach the gospel of peace, who bring glad tidings of good things!"
—*Romans 10:13-15* NKJV

At the center of God's will for our lives is His peace. Take time today to pray that it would be a constant in your life and in the lives of all those whose lives you touch.

PRAYING 2 THESSALONIANS 3:16 FOR YOURSELF

Father,

In the name of Jesus, I praise and thank You for Your mercy and Your peace bestowed on us through our Lord and Savior Jesus Christ. I pray that the Lord and Prince of Peace would continually grant me His peace—the peace He won for me on the Cross and is mine as a citizen of Your kingdom—in all situations, no matter what I face.

Lord, be with me in all things, under all circumstances, and with surety in my heart at all times.

Amen.

PRAYING 2 THESSALONIANS 3:16 FOR OTHERS

Father,

In the name of Jesus, I praise and thank You for Your mercy and Your peace bestowed upon all of us through our Lord and Savior Jesus Christ. I pray that the Lord and Prince of Peace would continually grant _____ His peace—the peace He won for _____ on the Cross and is _____'s as a citizen of Your kingdom—in all situations, no matter what _____ faces.

Lord, be with _____ in all things, under all circumstances, and with surety in _____'s heart at all times.

Amen.

PAUL'S PRAYER IN CONTEXT THROUGH VARIOUS TRANSLATIONS

2 Thessalonians 3:11-16 from the
New American Standard Bible (NASB)

We hear that some among you are leading an undisciplined life, doing no work at all, but acting like busybodies. Now such persons we command and exhort in the Lord Jesus Christ to work in quiet fashion and eat their own bread. But as for you, brethren, do not grow weary of doing good.

If anyone does not obey our instruction in this letter, take special note of that person and do not associate with him, so that he will be put to shame. Yet do not regard him as an enemy, but admonish him as a brother.

Now may the Lord of peace Himself continually grant you peace in every circumstance. The Lord be with you all!

2 Thessalonians 3:11-16 from the
International Standard Version (ISV)

We hear that some of you are living in idleness. You are not busy working—you are busy interfering in other people's lives! We order and encourage such people by the Lord Jesus Christ to do their work quietly and to earn their own living. Brothers, do not get tired of doing what is right.

If anyone does not obey what we say in this letter, take note of him. Have nothing to do with him so that he will feel ashamed. Yet, don't treat him like an enemy, but warn him like a brother. Now may the Lord of peace give you his peace at all times and in every way. May the Lord be with all of you.

2 Thessalonians 3:11-16 from the *Good News Translation* (GNT)

We say this because we hear that there are some people among you who live lazy lives and who do nothing except meddle in other people's business. In the name of the Lord Jesus Christ we command these people and warn them to lead orderly lives and work to earn their own living.

But you, brothers and sisters, must not get tired of doing good. It may be that someone there will not obey the message we send you in this letter. If so, take note of that person and have nothing to do with him or her, so that they will be ashamed. But do not treat them as an enemy; instead, warn them as a fellow-believer.

May the Lord himself, who is our source of peace, give you peace at all times and in every way. The Lord be with you all.

2 Thessalonians 3:11-16 from the *New Living Translation* (NLT)

We hear that some of you are living idle lives, refusing to work and wasting time meddling in other people's business. In the name of the Lord Jesus Christ, we appeal to such people—no, we command them: Settle down and get to work. Earn your own living. And I say to the rest of you, dear brothers and sisters, never get tired of doing good.

Take note of those who refuse to obey what we say in this letter. Stay away from them so they will be ashamed. Don't think of them as enemies, but speak to them as you would to a Christian who needs to be warned.

May the Lord of peace himself always give you his peace no matter what happens. The Lord be with you all.

2 Thessalonians 3:11-16 from the *Amplified Bible* (AMP)

We hear that some among you are disorderly [that they are passing their lives in idleness, neglectful of duty], being busy with other people's affairs instead of their own and doing no work.

Now we charge and exhort such persons [as ministers in Him exhorting those] in the Lord Jesus Christ (the Messiah) that they work in quietness and earn their own food and other necessities.

And as for you, brethren, do not become weary or lose heart in doing right [but continue in well-doing without weakening].

But if anyone [in the church] refuses to obey what we say in this letter, take note of that person and do not associate with him, so that he may be ashamed.

Do not regard him as an enemy, but simply admonish and warn him as [being still] a brother.

Now may the Lord of peace Himself grant you His peace (the peace of His kingdom) at all times and in all ways [under all circumstances and conditions, whatever comes]. The Lord [be] with you all.

chapter thirteen

MAKE MY FAITH EFFECTIVE

*I thank my God, making mention of thee always in my prayers,
hearing of thy love and faith, which thou hast toward the Lord
Jesus, and toward all saints; that the communication of thy
faith may become effectual by the acknowledging of every
good thing which is in you in Christ Jesus.*
Philemon 4-6

Paul wrote many letters, but his letter to Philemon is the only one written primarily to one specific person: an elder of "the church in [his] house" (Philemon 2 [insert added]) in Colossae. The subject of the letter is the return of Onesimus, a slave who ran away from Philemon, became a prisoner with Paul in Rome, heard the Gospel from Paul, and became a Christian. Now this newly won believer feels convicted to return to his former master and make amends for the sins he believes he has committed against him. In the letter Paul asks that Philemon and his congregation would welcome Onesimus back and forgive him as a new brother in Christ rather than resorting to the punishments normally inflicted on runaway slaves.

In the opening lines of this short letter, Paul prays for Philemon, acknowledging both his love for the family of God and his faith: *I thank God always when making mention of you in my prayers because I keep hearing reports of your love for all of the saints and the power of your loyal faith in our Lord Jesus Christ. I pray that the communication and sharing of your faith—the fellowship and partnership of your faith—will grow more and more effective through the knowledge, understanding, and acknowledgement of every good thing that is in us and that we can do in Christ Jesus* (Philemon 4-6, PARAPHRASED).

Paul's prayer here is unique in all of his writings. He doesn't pray that he would know his purpose and calling in life, that he would be inwardly strengthened by the Holy Spirit, or that he would receive new revelations of God's inheritance or power available to him. Instead, Paul prays that the effectiveness of Philemon's sharing of the Word of God would match and grow with his knowledge of who he was—and as a result, what he had—in Christ.

IN CHRIST

Some of the most profound and life-changing scriptures in the Bible are the "in Christ" scriptures. A good place for any Christian—young or maturing—to start studying the Bible is to find all of the "in Christ," "in Jesus," "in Him," "in Me," and "by Me" scriptures. They tell us who we are now in Christ.

> If anyone is *in Christ,* he is a new creation; old things have passed away; behold, all things have become new.... For He made Him who knew no sin to be sin for us, that we might become the righteousness of God *in Him.*
>
> —*2 Corinthians 5:17, 21* NKJV (emphasis added)

> There is therefore now no condemnation to those who are *in Christ Jesus,* who do not walk according to the flesh, but according to the Spirit. For the law of the

Spirit of life *in Christ Jesus* has made me free from the
law of sin and death.

—*Romans 8:1-2* NKJV (emphasis added)

All that has changed about you since you accepted Jesus Christ as
your Lord and Savior is wrapped up in your new life *in Christ.* As
when David looked upon Mephibosheth and saw in him his father,
Jonathan, so God the Father looks upon us and does not see our frail-
ties and sins. Rather, He sees Jesus, His beloved Son and our Redeemer.
Every action, every word has not been reclassified on the basis of our
relationship with the Cross of Christ. Whatever we have failed in, the
Cross has made up for, and whatever good thing we receive, the Cross
has made us worthy of. This is why Paul prayed for the Ephesians in
the first chapter of his letter to them that they would have the right to
know God, understand the hope of their calling in Him, the inheritance they have in Christ, and the dynamic power backing them up to
accomplish all God has called them out of the world to accomplish. We
owe all that we have as Christians to Jesus Christ.

> God, who is rich in mercy...made us alive together
> with Christ (by grace you have been saved), and *raised*
> *us up together, and made us sit together in the heavenly*
> *places in Christ Jesus,* that in the ages to come He
> might show the exceeding riches of His grace in His
> kindness toward us *in Christ Jesus.*
>
> —*Ephesians 2:4-7* NKJV (emphasis added)

According to this prayer, the more we understand of what we have in
Christ, who we are in Christ, and what we can accomplish in Christ,
the more effective our faith will be.

THE EFFECTIVE WORKING OF OUR FAITH

Once we begin to understand what it means to be "in Christ," we no longer have to struggle to believe God's promises for us today, not forgetting that we must do our part as well. While Jesus won so much for us on the Cross, we have access to it only as we "put on Christ."

> You have not so learned Christ, if indeed you have heard Him and have been taught by Him, as the truth is in Jesus: that you put off, concerning your former conduct, the old man which grows corrupt according to the deceitful lusts, and be renewed in the spirit of your mind, and that *you put on the new man* [Jesus] which was created according to God, in true right- eousness and holiness.
>
> —*Ephesians 4:20-24* NKJV (emphasis and insert added)

Take time to study and meditate on who you are "in Christ." Pray that each day would bring a fuller understanding of what that means. As you learn to live in that revelation, your faith will grow stronger and your communication of the Gospel to others will become more effec- tive. Take your seat at God's table—a seat purchased for you by Jesus, your Savior and Lord—and feast continually on God's goodness.

PRAYING PHILEMON 4-6 FOR YOURSELF

Father,

In the name of Jesus, I praise and thank You for Your faith and love in my life.

I pray that the communication of my faith to others would become increasingly effective. I pray that I would grow bolder as Your presence and guidance become more real in my life. And I pray that You would help me better know, understand, and live in the fulfillment of the potential that I have in Your Son, Jesus Christ.

Amen.

PRAYING PHILEMON 4-6 FOR OTHERS

Father,

In the name of Jesus, I praise and thank You for Your faith and love in the life of _____.

I pray that the communication of _____'s faith to others would become increasingly effective. I pray that _____ would grow bolder as Your presence and guidance become more real in _____ life. And I pray that you would help _____ better know, understand, and live in the fulfillment of the potential that _____ has in Your Son, Jesus Christ.

Amen.

PAUL'S PRAYER IN CONTEXT THROUGH VARIOUS TRANSLATIONS

Philemon 4-7 from the *New American Standard Bible* (NASB)

I thank my God always, making mention of you in my prayers, because I hear of your love and of the faith which you have toward the Lord Jesus and toward all the saints; and I pray that the fellowship of your faith may become effective through the knowledge of every good thing which is in you for Christ's sake. For I have come to have much joy and comfort in your love, because the hearts of the saints have been refreshed through you, brother.

Philemon 4-7 from the *New International Version* (NIV)

I always thank my God as I remember you in my prayers, because I hear about your faith in the Lord Jesus and your love for all the saints. I pray that you may be active in sharing your faith, so that you will have a full understanding of every good thing we have in Christ. Your love has given me great joy and encouragement, because you, brother, have refreshed the hearts of the saints.

Philemon 4-7 from the *International Standard Version* (ISV)

I always thank my God when I mention you in my prayers, because I keep hearing about your love and the faith that you have toward the Lord Jesus and for all the saints. I pray that the sharing of your faith may become effective as you fully acknowledge every blessing that is ours in Christ. For I have received considerable joy and encouragement from your love, because the hearts of the saints have been refreshed, brother, through you.

Philemon 4-7 from the *New Century Version* (NCV)

I always thank my God when I mention you in my prayers, because I hear about the love you have for all God's holy people and the faith you have in the Lord Jesus. I pray that the faith you share may make you understand every blessing we have in Christ. I have great joy and comfort, my brother, because the love you have shown to God's people has refreshed them.

Philemon 4-7 from the *Good News Translation* (GNT)

Brother Philemon, every time I pray, I mention you and give thanks to my God. For I hear of your love for all God's people and the faith you have in the Lord Jesus. My prayer is that our fellowship with you as believers will bring about a deeper understanding of every blessing which we have in our life in union with Christ. Your love, dear brother, has brought me great joy and much encouragement! You have cheered the hearts of all of God's people.

Philemon 4-7 from *the Message* (THE MESSAGE)

Every time your name comes up in my prayers, I say, "Oh, thank you, God!" I keep hearing of the love and faith you have for the Master Jesus, which brims over to other Christians. And I keep praying that this faith we hold in common keeps showing up in the good things we do, and that people recognize Christ in all of it. Friend, you have no idea how good your love makes me feel, doubly so when I see your hospitality to fellow believers.

Philemon 4-7 from the *New Living Translation* (NLT)

I always thank God when I pray for you, Philemon, because I keep hearing of your trust in the Lord Jesus and your love for all of God's people. You are generous because of your faith. And I am praying that you will really put your generosity to work, for in so doing you will come to an understanding of all the good things we can do for Christ. I myself have gained much joy and comfort from your love, my brother, because your kindness has so often refreshed the hearts of God's people.

Philemon 4-7 from the *Amplified Bible* (AMP)

I give thanks to my God for you always when I mention you in my prayers,

Because I continue to hear of your love and of your loyal faith which you have toward the Lord Jesus and [which you show] toward all the saints (God's consecrated people).

[And I pray] that the participation in and sharing of your faith may produce and promote full recognition and appreciation and understanding and precise knowledge of every good [thing] that is ours in [our identification with] Christ Jesus [and unto His glory].

For I have derived great joy and comfort and encouragement from your love, because the hearts of the saints [who are your fellow Christians] have been cheered and refreshed through you, [my] brother.

chapter fourteen

PRAYERS OF PRAISE AND THANKSGIVING

WE GLORIFY AND THANK YOU, FATHER

One of the most wonderful things about Paul's prayers is that they consistently begin with praise and worship and end with praise and thanksgiving. The most common ending to any of Paul's prayers could be summed up in the words, "To God be the glory. Amen." As those he was praying for received what he was requesting for them—insight and wisdom, strength from the inside out, excellence, guidance into His perfect will, unity, hope, abounding love, holiness, purpose, truth, patience, peace, or effective faith—his greatest desire was that their lives would ultimately glorify God.

In addition, many of Paul's prayers were beautifully cast expressions of praise and thanksgiving to God. They seem to flow forth almost spontaneously out of the fullness of Paul's love for Christ and his appreciation for what He had done for us.

TO HIM WHO HAS THE POWER TO ESTABLISH US

To him that is of power to stablish you according to
my gospel, and the preaching of Jesus Christ, according
to the revelation of the mystery, which was kept secret

since the world began, but now is made manifest, and
by the scriptures of the prophets, according to the
commandment of the everlasting God, made known to
all nations for the obedience of faith: To God only
wise, be glory through Jesus Christ for ever. Amen.

—*Romans 16:25-27*

In this closing prayer to the book of Romans, Paul praises God for
His wisdom and His willingness to share it with humanity. Paul praises
the God who revealed the Gospel to us through the preaching of Jesus
Christ, the teaching of Paul, and the revelation of His mysteries
through the indwelling of the Holy Spirit. This is reminiscent of what
John said in his first epistle:

> You have an anointing from the Holy One, and you
> all know....As for you, the anointing which you
> received from Him abides in you, and you have no
> need for anyone to teach you; but as His anointing
> teaches you about all things, and is true and is not a
> lie, and just as it has taught you, you abide in Him.

—*1 John 2:20, 27* NASB

Paul praises God for the magnificence of the mystery of holiness He
is making known to the universe through the church—the greatness of
the plan of salvation, the intricacy with which it appears in every book
of the Old Testament, the length of time it has been kept hidden, and
the wonder of all wonders that He would reveal it to human beings
rather than angels or other powers and principalities in the heavens.
What other wisdom in the universe could possibly measure up to that?

And for that reason, he closes in praise "to the only wise God, be glory through Jesus Christ forever. Amen."

> I thank my God always on your behalf, for the grace
> of God which is given you by Jesus Christ; that in
> every thing ye are enriched by him, in all utterance,
> and in all knowledge; even as the testimony of Christ
> was confirmed in you: So that ye come behind in no
> gift; waiting for the coming of our Lord Jesus Christ:
> Who shall also confirm you unto the end, that ye may
> be blameless in the day of our Lord Jesus Christ. God
> is faithful, by whom ye were called unto the fellowship
> of his Son Jesus Christ our Lord.
>
> —*1 Corinthians 1:4-9*

Paul wrote his first letter to the Corinthians in response to problems he learned they were having in their walk with Christ. He could have opened his letter to them with a rebuke for their foolishness. Instead, he chooses to begin his letter with praise for the God who called them into light in the first place and who was still doing remarkable things through them. He praises the God of grace who did not immediately call down judgment for their mistakes, but instead corrected them so they could repent and be restored. He praised the God whose testimony was still seen in them and who enabled them to "come behind in no gift," and would see them blameless and holy by the time His Son returned to the earth. Confronted by their unfaithfulness, Paul points first to God's faithfulness and the continued hope they have in Him. Paul wisely realized that it is not the judgment of God that brings people back to Him, but "the kindness of God leads you to repentance" (Romans 2:4 NASB).

Just as Paul wrote in his last letter to Timothy:

If we are faithless,
He remains faithful;
He cannot deny Himself.

—2 Timothy 2:13 NKJV

Because God cannot deny His own nature, He remains faithful even when we are not.

PRAISE BE TO THE GOD OF ALL COMFORT AND MERCIES

In the first verses of his second letter to the Corinthians, Paul calls their attention to the God of all comfort and mercy:

Blessed be God, even the Father of our Lord Jesus Christ,
the Father of mercies, and the God of all comfort;
Who comforteth us in all our tribulation, that we may
be able to comfort them which are in any trouble, by
the comfort wherewith we ourselves are comforted of
God. For as the sufferings of Christ abound in us, so
our consolation also aboundeth by Christ.

—2 Corinthians 1:3-5

Paul's emphasis is on the goodness of God—His gifts, His fruit, and His comfort and mercies. We are blessed so that we can be blessings to others. What we have suffered in, what mistakes we have made, and the consolation we have received from Christ make us stronger and better able to reach out with the love of God to others. In this letter, much more than the first, Paul was calling the Corinthians not only to correct their mistakes but also to walk in maturity so that they could be a blessing to others in Achaia.

Again, later in this same letter, Paul offers other praises to God in the midst of his writing and teaching:

> Thanks be to God, who always leads us in triumphal procession in Christ and through us spreads everywhere the fragrance of the knowledge of him.
>
> —*2 Corinthians 2:14* NIV

> Thanks be unto God for his unspeakable gift.
>
> —*2 Corinthians 9:15*

Paul thanks God for the miraculous gift of salvation and triumph in Christ. God's plan is and has always been that His greatness and the knowledge of Him would be shown to the world through us. What a privilege to be called to show His glory to the universe!

PAUL THANKS GOD FOR THE FAITHFULNESS OF OTHERS

In the introductions to his letters to the Thessalonians, Paul thanks God again for what has turned out to be his greatest joy: that those he shared the Gospel with would remain faithful to it and prosper in it!

> We [Timothy, Silvanus, and Paul] give thanks to God always for you all, making mention of you in our prayers; remembering without ceasing your work of faith, and labour of love, and patience of hope in our

Lord Jesus Christ, in the sight of God and our Father;
knowing, brethren beloved, your election of God.

—*1 Thessalonians 1:2-4* [insert added]

For this cause also thank we God without ceasing,
because, when ye received the word of God which ye
heard of us, ye received it not as the word of men, but
as it is in truth, the word of God, which effectually
worketh also in you that believe.

—*1 Thessalonians 2:13*

In this same letter, Paul calls those who have heard the Gospel from
him and remain faithful his crown:

What is our hope, or joy, or crown of rejoicing? Is it
not even you in the presence of our Lord Jesus Christ
at His coming? *For you are our glory and joy.*

—*1 Thessalonians 2:19-20* NKJV (emphasis added)

And again a few verses later, Paul says that in fulfilling his God-given
purpose, he has found real life—true joy and satisfaction—in those
who have remained faithful and stand firm in the Lord.

For this reason, brethren, in all our distress and affliction we were comforted about you through your faith;
for now we really live, if you stand firm in the Lord.

—*1 Thessalonians 3:7-8* NASB (emphasis added)

What a wonderful thing it must have been for Paul when he heard
that the Word of God was spreading in Macedonia far beyond the
reach of his own preaching. He knew that the faithfulness of the

Thessalonians was God's doing and not his own. And once again, God was to be praised.

GLORY TO GOD FOR HIS GREATNESS

In 1 Timothy, Paul stops twice to give thanks to God for the wonder of who He is:

> Unto the King eternal, immortal, invisible, the only wise God, be honour and glory for ever and ever. Amen.
>
> —*1 Timothy 1:17*

> In his times he shall shew, who is the blessed and only Potentate, the King of kings, and Lord of lords; Who only hath immortality, dwelling in the light which no man can approach unto; whom no man hath seen, nor can see: to whom be honour and power everlasting. Amen.
>
> —*1 Timothy 6:15-16*

In both of these prayers, Paul gives glory to the King of all, the Supreme Ruler of the universe without equal, God the Father. Both these passages follow Paul's discussions of the wonders of being called to be ministers of the Gospel of Christ and agents of God's salvation to the earth. Paul's awe of God only increased as he grew in his understanding of God's nature and His redemptive work on behalf of mankind.

Paul praises Him as the eternal, immortal, and invisible One, the only wise God, the blessed and only Potentate, the King of kings and the Lord of lords. He applauds the majesty which no mortal can look on and live because of His purity and Holiness, yet the One who sent

His Son to save us, and whose will it is that His manifest wisdom would be made known to the universe through us, His Church.

PRESSING THROUGH TO PRAISE

While Paul faced many hardships in his ministry, more than most of us will ever dream of facing, he always pushed through in his prayers to the point of praising God again for His glory and wisdom. He stayed in prayer until God so filled his heart that nothing else could pour forth but worship, praise, and thanksgiving.

This is perhaps the greatest insight we can gain from the prayers of Paul. Prayer is not a duty but a door that opens our lives to God's freedom in the Spirit.

PRAISING AND WORSHIPING GOD ACCORDING TO PAUL'S PRAYERS

Father,

You alone have the power to establish all of us according to the Good News of Christ. You have chosen to reveal through the Church the mystery of Your manifold wisdom, a secret You kept from the beginning of Creation until the day you raised Jesus from the dead. You now are making that wisdom manifest to the entire universe through those of us who obey You. To You, the only wise God, be glory through Christ Jesus forevermore.

You, Father, through the grace of our Lord and Savior Jesus Christ have enriched us in all utterance and knowledge and examples and testimonies to the greatness of Jesus. Therefore we will come behind in no gift. You have enabled us to be steadfast and blameless until the day Jesus returns for us. You are faithful who has called us into the fellowship of Your Son, Jesus Christ our Lord.

You always cause us to triumph in Your Son and You raise the aroma of salvation in every place we preach of You and bring people to know You. You have enabled each of us to be ministers and ambassadors of Your grace regardless of our pasts and abilities.

To You, the only wise God, the King eternal, immortal, unseeable by human eyes, who dwells in the light which no one can approach, who is the blessed and only Potentate, the King of kings, and the Lord of lords, be the glory through Christ Jesus, the Church, and my life forever and ever.

In Jesus' name. Amen

PAUL'S PRAYERS OF PRAISE AND WORSHIP IN VARIOUS TRANSLATIONS

Romans 16:25-27 from the *New Century Version* (NCV)

Glory to God who can make you strong in faith by the Good News that I tell people and by the message about Jesus Christ. The message about Christ is the secret that was hidden for long ages past but is now made known. It has been made clear through the writings of the prophets. And by the command of the eternal God it is made known to all nations that they might believe and obey. To the only wise God be glory forever through Jesus Christ! Amen.

Romans 16:25-27 from the *Contemporary English Version* (CEV)

Praise God! He can make you strong by means of my good news, which is the message about Jesus Christ. For ages and ages this message was kept secret, but now at last it has been told. The eternal God commanded his prophets to write about the good news, so that all nations would obey and have faith. And now, because of Jesus Christ, we can praise the only wise God forever! Amen.

Romans 16:25-27 from *the Message* (THE MESSAGE)

All of our praise rises to the One who is strong enough to make you strong, exactly as preached in Jesus Christ, precisely as revealed in the mystery kept secret for so long but now an open book through the prophetic Scriptures. All the nations of the world can now know the truth and be brought into obedient belief, carrying out the orders of God, who got all this started, down to the very last letter.

All our praise is focused through Jesus on this incomparably wise God! Yes!

1 Corinthians 1:4-9 from the *New International Version* (NIV)

I always thank God for you because of his grace given you in Christ Jesus. For in him you have been enriched in every way—in all your speaking and in all your knowledge—because our testimony about Christ was confirmed in you. Therefore you do not lack any spiritual gift as you eagerly wait for our Lord Jesus Christ to be revealed. He will keep you strong to the end, so that you will be blameless on the day of our Lord

Jesus Christ. God, who has called you into fellowship with his Son Jesus Christ our Lord, is faithful.

1 Corinthians 1:4-9 from the *New Living Translation* (NLT)

I can never stop thanking God for all the generous gifts he has given you, now that you belong to Christ Jesus. He has enriched your church with the gifts of eloquence and every kind of knowledge. This shows that what I told you about Christ is true. Now you have every spiritual gift you need as you eagerly wait for the return of our Lord Jesus Christ. He will keep you strong right up to the end, and he will keep you free from all blame on the great day when our Lord Jesus Christ returns. God will surely do this for you, for he always does just what he says, and he is the one who invited you into this wonderful friendship with his Son, Jesus Christ our Lord.

2 Corinthians 1:3-5 from the *New King James Version* (NKJV)

Blessed be the God and Father of our Lord Jesus Christ, the Father of mercies and God of all comfort, who comforts us in all our tribulation, that we may be able to comfort those who are in any trouble, with the comfort with which we ourselves are comforted by God. For as the sufferings of Christ abound in us, so our consolation also abounds through Christ.

2 Corinthians 1:3-5 from the *Good News Translation* (GNT)

Let us give thanks to the God and Father of our Lord Jesus Christ, the merciful Father, the God from whom all help comes! He helps us in all our troubles, so that we are able to help others who have all kinds of troubles, using the same help that we ourselves have received from God. Just as we have a share in Christ's many sufferings, so also through Christ we share in God's great help.

1 Thessalonians 1:2-4 from the
International Standard Version (ISV)

We always thank God for all of you when we mention you in our prayers. In the presence of our God and Father, we constantly remember how your faith is active, your love is hard at work, and your hope in our Lord Jesus Christ is enduring. Brothers whom God loves, we know that he has chosen you.

1 Thessalonians 1:2-4 from the *Good New Translation* (GNT)

We always thank God for you all and always mention you in our prayers. For we remember before our God and Father how you put your faith into practice, how your love made you work so hard, and how your hope in our Lord Jesus Christ is firm. Our brothers and sisters, we know that God loves you and has chosen you to be his own.

1 Thessalonians 2:13 from the *International Standard Version* (ISV)

Here is another reason why we constantly give thanks to God: When you received God's word, which you heard from us, you did not accept it as the word of humans but for what it really is—the word of God, which is at work in you who believe.

1 Thessalonians 2:13 from *the Message* (THE MESSAGE)

Now we look back on all this and thank God, an artesian well of thanks! When you got the Message of God we preached, you didn't pass it off as just one more human opinion, but you took it to heart as God's true word to you, which it is, God himself at work in you believers!

1 Timothy 1:17 from the *New American Standard Bible* (NASB)

Now to the King eternal, immortal, invisible, the only God, be honor and glory forever and ever. Amen.

1 Timothy 1:17 from *the Message* (THE MESSAGE)

Deep honor and bright glory to the King of All Time—One God, Immortal, Invisible, ever and always. Oh, yes!

1 Timothy 1:17 from the *New Century Version* (NCV)

To the King that rules forever, who will never die, who cannot be seen, the only God, be honor and glory forever and ever. Amen.

1 Timothy 6:13-16 from the *New American Standard Bible* (NASB)

I charge you...that you keep the commandment...which He will bring about at the proper time—He who is the blessed and only Sovereign, the King of kings and Lord of lords, who alone possesses immortality and dwells in unapproachable light, whom no man has seen or can see. To Him be honor and eternal dominion! Amen.

1 Timothy 6:15-16 from the *International Standard Version* (ISV)

At the right time God will make him known. He is the blessed and only Ruler, the King of kings and Lord of lords. He alone has endless life and lives in inaccessible light. No one has ever seen him, nor can anyone see him. Honor and eternal power belong to him! Amen.

1 Timothy 6:15-16 from *the Message* (THE MESSAGE)

He'll show up right on time, his arrival guaranteed by the Blessed and Undisputed Ruler, High King, High God. He's the only one death can't touch, his light so bright no one can get close. He's never been seen by human eyes—human eyes can't take him in! Honor to him, and eternal rule! Oh, yes.

PRAYING THE PRAYERS OF PAUL

A Prayer for Wisdom and Revelation

PRAYING EPHESIANS 1:15-23 FOR YOURSELF

Father,

In the name of Jesus, I praise and thank You for all of the spiritual gifts You have bestowed upon me in Christ Jesus. I thank You that You have adopted me as Your child, that you have forgiven my sins, that You have promised to let me know the purposes for which You saved me, and the greatness of the inheritance You have prepared for me to accomplish that purpose. I also praise and thank You for sealing me with Your Holy Spirit to live within me and guide me—that Your fullness will be realized in my life as I follow and learn from Him day by day.

Because of these great blessings, Father, I pray that You would give me a spirit of revelation and knowledge in knowing You. Open the eyes of my understanding so that I would know the hope of Your calling. Help me to understand the riches of the glory of Your great inheritance to me through Jesus Christ because I have believed on and trust in You. I pray that I would come to understand the exceedingly great power You have made available to me to accomplish what You have called me to do.

Father, I thank You that all these things are accomplished according to Your exceedingly great strength—the very power by which You sent Your Son, Jesus, to earth to die on the Cross for my sins, and by which You raised Him from the dead to sit at Your right hand in the heavens, far above any other ruler, authority, power, or kingdom; above every name that is named, not only in this world, but in the world to come; with all things under His feet;

and as the head of all parts of the universal Church, which is His Body on the earth, left here to accomplish His goals and purposes as His fullness to all humankind.

Amen.

PRAYING EPHESIANS 1:15-23 FOR OTHERS

Father,

In the name of Jesus, I praise and thank You for all of the spiritual gifts You have bestowed upon _____ in Christ Jesus. I thank You that You have adopted _____ as Your own child, and that You have forgiven all of _____ sins. I thank You for all of Your promises, that You will reveal to _____, Your divine purpose and calling for _____ life, and that _____ would understand the greatness of the inheritance You have prepared for _____ to accomplish that purpose and calling. I also praise and thank You for sealing _____ with Your Holy Spirit to live within _____ and guide _____ into all of Your fullness.

Because of these great blessings, Father, I pray that You will give _____ a spirit of revelation and knowledge in knowing You. Open _____'s eyes of understanding so that _____ would know the full hope of Your calling. Help _____ to understand the riches of the glory of Your great inheritance for _____ through Jesus Christ because _____ has believed on and trusted in You. I pray that _____ would come to understand the exceedingly great power You have made available to _____ to accomplish what You have called _____ to do on this earth.

Father: I thank You that all of these requests will be accomplished according to Your exceedingly great power—the very power by which You sent Your Son, Jesus, to the earth to die on the Cross for our sins, and by which You raised Him from the dead to sit at Your right hand in the heavens, far above any other ruler, authority, power, or kingdom; above every name that is named, not only in this world, but in the world to come; with all things under His feet; and as the head of all parts of the universal Church, which is His Body on the earth, left here to accomplish His goals and purposes as His fullness to all humankind.

Amen.

A Prayer for Spiritual Strength

PRAYING EPHESIANS 3:14-21 FOR YOURSELF

Father,

In the name of Jesus, I praise and thank You that You saved me for a purpose, and that You have a plan for my life that exceeds my most imaginative hopes and dreams. For that reason, Father, I bow my knee to You, the God of heaven and earth from whom Your whole family receives our name. I pray that by Your glorious riches You would strengthen me on the inside through the power of Your Holy Spirit and that Christ would truly live in my heart and live through me by my faith in You.

Help me to understand with all of the saints the breadth, length, depth, and height of Your love which surpasses all knowledge. Fill me with all of Your fullness—Your wisdom, strength, and power—so that I would live constantly to Your glory!

Now unto You, Father, who is able to do exceedingly far above all that I ask or can imagine, be the glory in the church through Christ Jesus throughout all the ages and forever.

Amen.

PRAYING EPHESIANS 3:14-21 FOR OTHERS

Father,

In the name of Jesus, I praise and thank You that You saved _____ for a special purpose, and that You have a plan for _____ life that exceeds anything _____ has ever imagined or hoped for. For this reason, I bow my knee to You, the God from whom Your whole family in heaven and on earth have received our name. I pray that by Your glorious riches You would strengthen _____ on the inside through the power of Your Holy Spirit and that Christ would truly live in _____'s heart and live through _____ by faith in You.

Help _____ to understand with all of the saints the breadth, length, depth, and height of Your love which surpasses all knowledge. Fill _____ with all of Your fullness that Your wisdom, strength, power, and fullness would be in _____ to Your glory!

Now unto You, Father, who is able to do exceedingly far above all that any of us can ask or imagine, be the glory in the church through Christ Jesus throughout all the ages and forever.

Amen.

A Prayer for Guidance

PRAYING PHILIPPIANS 1:9-11 FOR YOURSELF

Father,

In the name of Jesus, I pray that Your love that was shed abroad in my heart by the Holy Spirit would abound and grow more and more, strengthening my knowledge of You and of the things You have called me to do, in the discernment and spiritual insight of the Holy Spirit.

I pray that I can prove Your excellence by always knowing the right things to do and doing them with excellence, and that I will remain sincere, genuine, and real in all my encounters with others and free from blame or even the appearance of evil until the day of Jesus Christ's return.

Allow this to also lead to my overflowing in the fruits of Your righteousness, which I have because of Jesus Christ, that all of this would make me a constant glory and praise to You under all circumstances and in all things.

Amen.

PRAYING PHILIPPIANS 1:9-11 FOR OTHERS

Father,

In the name of Jesus, I pray that Your love that was shed abroad in _____'s heart by the Holy Spirit would abound and grow more and more, strengthening _____'s knowledge of You and of the things You have called _____ to do, in the discernment and spiritual insight of the Holy Spirit.

I pray that _____ can prove Your excellence by always knowing the right things to do and doing them with excellence, and that _____ will remain sincere, genuine, and real in all his/her encounters with others and free from blame or even the appearance of evil until the day of Jesus Christ's return.

Allow this to also lead to _____ overflowing in the fruits of Your righteousness, which I have because of Jesus Christ, that all of this would make _____ a constant glory and praise to You under all circumstances and in all things.

Amen.

A Prayer for Fulfilling God's Perfect Will

PRAYING COLOSSIANS 1:9-12 FOR YOURSELF

Father,

In the name of Jesus, I praise and thank You for Your faithfulness to continue the good work You began in me until that day You call me home to be with You. Because of this, Father, I ask that You further reveal to me the calling and purpose for my life, making it more and more real to me so I know how to walk it out and also have the spiritual insight into its timing and application; and that in every situation I would clearly see Your will and know how to pursue it effectively in order to fulfill Your perfect will for my life.

I pray that each step I take in working out Your plan would be pleasing to You and that all of my efforts would overflow with fruitfulness. May each step I take increase my knowledge of You and help me to grow closer to You.

I pray that I would be continually growing in Your strength according to Your power to the point that nothing can phase me and I can endure anything that might come at me with joy and thanksgiving for what You have done for me, what You are currently doing, and what You are yet to do because, through Jesus, You have made me fit to take part in the inheritance laid up for all of the saints who walk in Your light.

Amen.

PRAYING COLOSSIANS 1:9-12 FOR OTHERS

Father,

In the name of Jesus, I praise and thank You for Your faithfulness to continue the good work you began in _____ until that day You call _____ home to be with You. Because of this, Father, I ask that You further reveal to _____ the calling and purpose for _____ life, making it more and more real to _____ so _____ knows how to walk it out and also will see when and how to achieve it through the insight of the Holy Spirit; and that in every situation _____ would clearly see Your will and know how to pursue it effectively to fulfilling Your perfect will for _____ life.

I pray that each step that _____ takes in working out Your plan would be pleasing to You and that all of _____'s efforts would overflow with fruitfulness. May each step _____ takes increase _____ knowledge of You and help _____ grow closer to You.

I also pray that _____ would be strengthened according to Your power to the point that nothing could discourage _____ so that _____ can endure anything that might come with joy and thanksgiving for all that You have done, all that You are currently doing, and all that You have yet to do, because, through Jesus, You have made _____ fit to take part in the inheritance laid up for all of the saints who walk in Your light.

Amen.

A Prayer for Unity

PRAYING ROMANS 15:5-6 FOR YOURSELF

Heavenly Father,

I know that it is by Your Spirit that I have the power to forgive, and that it is through the fruit of Your Spirit that I can overcome the challenges of life and become an encouragement to others. I thank You that You give me the power to be a unifier, a reconciler, and a peacemaker so that others might see Your love and grace in my everyday life.

Therefore, Lord, I pray that by Your divine power I would be a unifier and peacemaker today and that You will use me to bring a spirit of unity for Your will wherever I go and in whatever I do, whether it be at work, at church, in my community, or even in my own family. I pray this so that with one heart and one mouth we may all bring glory to You, the Father of our Lord and Savior Jesus Christ.

In Jesus' name. Amen

PRAYING ROMANS 15:5-6 FOR YOUR LOVED ONES, YOUR CHURCH, YOUR ORGANIZATION OR BUSINESS, OR YOUR CITY

Heavenly Father,

I know that it is by Your Spirit that we have the power to forgive, and that it is through the fruit of Your Spirit that we can overcome the challenges of life and become encouragers to others around us. I thank You that You have called us as Christians to be unifiers, reconcilers, and peacemakers on this earth as a display of Your love and grace in our everyday lives. I also thank You for giving us an example of true unity in Your relationship with Your Son, Jesus, as He walked upon this earth and that we can be one as You and He were one because of His prayers for us in John 17.

For this reason, Father, I pray for unity for _____. I pray that You would not only use _____ to be a unifier, reconciler, and peacemaker but that the Holy Spirit would also be present with _____ every day to help _____ overcome with Your joy and encourage others as _____ follows Jesus. I pray that in unity with one heart and one mouth _____ may glorify You, the Father of our Lord and Savior Jesus Christ.

In Jesus' name. Amen

A Prayer for Hope

PRAYING ROMANS 15:13 FOR YOURSELF

Father,

In Jesus' name I give thanks that You are the God of hope and that by drawing near to You and coming to know You better each day, You are causing overflowing hope to grow in my heart so that I might experience the depths of Your peace and the height of Your joy, even as I learn to trust You more fully every day, by the power of the Holy Spirit.

Thank You, Lord, that the more I learn to trust in You, the more the Holy Spirit, by His power, opens the floodgates of Your hope into my life. I receive Your anointing of hope right now.

Amen.

PRAYING ROMANS 15:13 FOR OTHERS

Father,

Thank You that the more _____ learns to trust in You, the more the Holy Spirit, by His power, opens the floodgates of Your hope into _____ life. Please help _____ by giving _____ Your anointing of hope right now.

In Jesus' name I give thanks that You are the God of hope and that You long for _____ to know You and trust You more fully so that Your hope may abound in _____'s life. I pray that You will draw _____ near to You, Lord, and that _____ will come to know You better and better each day. As _____ does, I thank You for causing overflowing hope to grow in _____ heart so that _____ may experience more and more of Your joy and peace.

Amen.

A Prayer for Abounding Love

PRAYING 1 THESSALONIANS 3:11-13
FOR YOURSELF

Father

In the name of Jesus, I pray that You would increase to overflowing Your love shed abroad in my heart through the Holy Spirit toward other believers and also those whom I encounter daily who have not yet come to know You.

May my heart be established in Your holiness, blameless before You unto the day Jesus returns to this earth with all of the saints who have gone on before.

Amen.

PRAYING 1 THESSALONIANS 3:11-13
FOR OTHERS

Father,

In the name of Jesus, I pray that You would increase to abounding the love shed abroad in _____'s heart through Your Holy Spirit toward other believers in _____ church and area and also those whom _____ encounters daily who have not yet come to know You.

May _____'s heart be established in Your holiness, blameless before You until the day Jesus returns to this earth with all of the saints who have gone on before.

Amen.

A Prayer for Total Sanctification

PRAYING 1 THESSALONIANS 5:23
FOR YOURSELF

Father,

In the name of Jesus, I praise and thank You for being the God of Peace. I pray that You would sanctify me completely from my inner spirit to my outer actions, making my life stand out to others as an example of Your grace, mercy, love, and righteousness. Father, help me to walk worthy of my heavenly citizenship even as Jesus has made me worthy through His sacrifice on the Cross.

I pray that my entire spirit, soul, and body would be sanctified and complete for the purpose to which You have called me. That I would live blamelessly, above reproach, and without any appearance of evil—fit for Your use in all things and ready to spread Your kingdom upon the earth until the return of Your Son, my Lord and Savior Jesus Christ.

Now unto You, who called me, be the glory for ever and ever, even as You will be faithful to walk out and make certain Your sanctification and will are fulfilled in my life.

Amen.

PRAYING 1 THESSALONIANS 5:23 FOR YOUR LOVED ONES

Father,

In the name of Jesus, I praise and thank You for being the God of Peace. I pray that You would sanctify _____ completely from _____ inner spirit to _____ outer actions, making _____'s life stand out to others as an example of Your grace, mercy, love, and righteousness. Father, I pray that _____ would walk worthy of Your heavenly calling for _____ and _____ citizenship in Your kingdom.

I pray that _____'s entire spirit, soul, and body be sanctified and complete for the purpose to which You have called _____. I also pray that _____ would live blamelessly, above reproach, and without any appearance of evil and would be fit for Your use in all things. That _____ would fervently spread Your kingdom upon the earth until the return of Your Son, our Lord and Savior Jesus Christ.

Now unto You, who called _____, be the glory for ever and ever, even as You will be faithful to walk out and make certain Your sanctification and will in _____'s life.

Amen.

A Prayer to Fulfill Your Purpose

PRAYING 2 THESSALONIANS 1:11-12
FOR YOURSELF

Father,

In the name of Jesus, I praise and thank You for the faith and love You have put into me and what they are doing to transform my world into Your kingdom on earth. I thank You also for the promise that Your Son will come again soon, and that our victory on the earth over the devil and his followers is assured. Because of these promises and gifts, I pray that I would be counted worthy—and able to accomplish—the calling Your life has given me on the earth.

May my accomplishment of that calling and purpose be to Your full pleasure; I pray that I would leave no area of life unfilled in its accomplishment and that all whom I touch would come to greater wholeness through coming in contact with me.

May all of the things I have set my faith to accomplish—the things You have called me to do and the good that I have seen that needs to be done in this world—be achieved through Your power and to Your glory.

I pray that Your glory would encompass me on this earth as I experience Your presence and pleasure as a testimony that I am living the way You have called me to live.

Now let all of these things happen according to Your grace and that of Your Son, my Lord and Savior, Jesus Christ.

Amen.

PRAYING 2 THESSALONIANS 1:11-12
FOR OTHERS

Father,

In the name of Jesus, I praise and thank You for the faith and love active in the life of _____ and what it is doing to bring Your kingdom to this earth. I thank You also for the promise that Your Son will come again soon, and that our victory on the earth over the devil and his followers is assured. Because of these promises and gifts, I pray that _____ would be counted worthy—and able to accomplish—the calling You have given _____ on the earth;

May _____'s accomplishment of that calling and purpose be to Your full pleasure; that no part of _____ life would be unfulfilled and that all whom _____ touches in _____ walk with You would come to greater wholeness;

May all of the things _____ has set _____ faith to accomplish— the things You have called _____ to do and the good that _____ has seen that needs to be done in this world—be achieved through Your power and to Your glory.

I pray that Your glory would encompass _____ on this earth as _____ experiences Your presence and pleasure as a testimony that _____ is living the way You have called _____ to live.

Now let all of these things happen according to Your grace and that of Your Son, my Lord and Savior, Jesus Christ.

Amen.

A Prayer for Steadfastness in the Truth

PRAYING 2 THESSALONIANS 2:16-17 FOR YOURSELF

Father,

In the name of Jesus, I pray that You—the Father of our Lord Jesus Christ—who first loved me and by Your grace has given me everlasting comfort and consolation through the indwelling of Your Holy Spirit, would infuse me with Your truth and give me a good, effective, and solid hope in what You have promised me in Your Word and what You have called me individually to accomplish during my time on the earth. I pray that You would comfort my heart with Your grace and presence, and establish and firmly found me in every good word of Your truth so that I understand every aspect of it, can base my life upon it, and communicate it to others.

Establish and firmly found me in every good action or work of Your truth so that I may walk in every aspect of it and effectively reach out to others in all that I do.

Amen.

PRAYING 2 THESSALONIANS 2:16-17
FOR OTHERS

Father,

*In the name of Jesus, I pray that You—the Father of our Lord
Jesus Christ—who first loved us and by Your grace has given us
everlasting comfort and consolation through the indwelling of Your
Holy Spirit, would infuse _____ with Your truth and give _____
a good, effective, and solid hope in what You have promised
_____ in Your Word and what You have each of us, both individually and corporately, to accomplish during our time on the earth.
I pray that You would comfort _____'s heart with Your grace and
presence and establish and firmly found _____ in every good
word of Your truth so that _____ understands every aspect of it,
can base _____ life upon it, and communicate it to others.*

*Establish and firmly found _____ in every good action or work of
Your truth so that _____ can walk in every aspect of it and effectively reach out to others in all that _____ does.*

Amen.

A Prayer for Patience

PRAYING 2 THESSALONIANS 3:5
FOR YOURSELF

Father,

In the name of Jesus, I praise and thank You for being the God of love, the God of hope, and the God of peace. Because of these, I pray that You would direct my heart into—strengthen my inner person with—Your eternal love, so that I might, with the patience of Christ, endure the race You have set before me to its accomplishment, and that I might stick to it faithfully until the day of Christ.

Amen.

PRAYING 2 THESSALONIANS 3:5 FOR OTHERS

Father,

In the name of Jesus, I praise and thank You for being the God of love, the God of hope, and the God of peace. Because of these, I pray that You would direct _____'s heart into—strengthen _____ inner person with—Your eternal love, so that _____ might, with the patience of Christ, endure the race You have set before _____ to its accomplishment, and that _____ would stick faithfully to it until the day of Christ.

Amen.

A Prayer for His Peace

PRAYING 2 THESSALONIANS 3:16
FOR YOURSELF

Father,

In the name of Jesus, I praise and thank You for Your mercy and Your peace bestowed on us through our Lord and Savior Jesus Christ. I pray that the Lord and Prince of Peace would:

1. *Continually grant me His peace—the peace He won for me on the Cross and is mine as a citizen of Your kingdom—in all situations, no matter what I face.*

2. *Be with me in all things, under all circumstances, and with surety in my heart at all times.*

Amen.

PRAYING 2 THESSALONIANS 3:16 FOR OTHERS

Father,

In the name of Jesus, I praise and thank You for Your mercy and Your peace bestowed upon all of us through our Lord and Savior Jesus Christ. I pray that the Lord and Prince of Peace would:

1. *Continually grant _____ His peace—the peace He won for _____ on the Cross and is _____'s as a citizen of Your kingdom—in all situations, no matter what _____ faces.*

2. *Be with _____ in all things, under all circumstances, and with surety in _____'s heart at all times.*

Amen.

A Prayer for Effective Faith

PRAYING PHILEMON 4-6 FOR YOURSELF

Father,

In the name of Jesus, I praise and thank You for Your faith and love in my life.

I pray that the communication of my faith to others would become increasingly effective. I pray that I would grow bolder as Your presence and guidance become more real in my life. And I pray that You would help me better know, understand, and live in the fulfillment of the potential that I have in Your Son, Jesus Christ.

Amen.

PRAYING PHILEMON 4-6 FOR OTHERS

Father,

In the name of Jesus, I praise and thank You for Your faith and love in the life of _____.

I pray that the communication of _____'s faith to others would become increasingly effective. I pray that _____ would grow bolder as Your presence and guidance become more real in _____ life. And I pray that you would help _____ better know, understand, and live in the fulfillment of the potential that _____ has in Your Son, Jesus Christ.

Amen.

A Prayer of Praise and Thanksgiving

Father,

You alone have the power to establish all of us according to the Good News of Christ. You have chosen to reveal through the Church the mystery of Your manifold wisdom, a secret You kept from the beginning of Creation until the day You raised Jesus from the dead. You now are making that wisdom manifest to the entire universe through those of us who obey You. To You, the only wise God, be glory through Christ Jesus forever more.

You, Father, who through the grace of our Lord and Savior Jesus Christ, have enriched us in all utterance and knowledge and examples and testimonies to the greatness of Jesus. Therefore we will come behind in no gift. You have enabled us to be steadfast and blameless until the day Jesus returns for us. You are faithful who has called us into the fellowship of Your Son Jesus Christ our Lord.

You always cause us to triumph in Your Son and You raise the aroma of salvation in every place we preach of You and bring people to know You. You have enabled each of us to be ministers and ambassadors of Your grace regardless of our pasts and abilities.

To you, the only wise God, the King eternal, immortal, unseeable by human eyes, who dwells in the light which no one can approach, who is the blessed and only Potentate, the King of kings, and the Lord of lords, be the glory through Christ Jesus, the Church, and my life forever and ever.

In Jesus' name. Amen

Part Three

THE LIFE OF PAUL

PAUL'S LIFE AND MINISTRY

You have heard of my former conduct in Judaism, how I
persecuted the church of God beyond measure and tried to
destroy it. And I advanced in Judaism beyond many of my
contemporaries in my own nation, being more exceedingly
zealous for the traditions of my fathers. But...it pleased
God, who separated me from my mother's womb and
called me through His grace, to reveal His Son in me,
that I might preach Him among the Gentiles.

Galatians 1:13-16 NKJV

From what the Bible and history tell us of Paul, he was born in the
city of Tarsus in the Roman province of Cicilia sometime in the decade
following the birth of Jesus. He was the son of a Pharisee and raised to
be a Pharisee. He was also born a Roman citizen, suggesting that
someone in his ancestry had done some service for the Romans worthy
of such a reward. According to Jewish tradition, he was "circumcised
the eighth day, of the stock of Israel, of the tribe of Benjamin, an
Hebrew of the Hebrews" (Philippians 3:5). The name he was given was
that of another famous Benjamite: Saul, the first king of Israel.

Tarsus was a university town, a center of local commerce, and the
capital of the province. As such it was also home to people of many
different cultures. Paul grew up speaking and writing Greek as well as
Hebrew, and he must have been exposed to Greek and Roman philoso-
phy as well as other Western ways in his education.

While little is known of Saul's earliest years, it seems evident that his
education began early—probably under his father's tutelage and in the
local synagogue school. As a youth, Paul picked up a talent for leather

working and tent making, probably also from his father. It was a skill that would serve him well in years to come.

At some point Paul outgrew Tarsus and traveled to Jerusalem—in order to further his education as a rabbi and a Pharisee. (It was later in his ministry that his nephew, ["his sister's son," (See Acts 23:16.)] warned him that the religious leaders lay in wait to assassinate him.) Saul must have been an excellent student because only the best were privileged to learn "at the feet of Gamaliel" (Acts 22:3), who was "a teacher of the law held in respect by all the people" (Acts 5:34 NKJV).

It would seem that young Saul was an ambitious social climber who used his heritage and upbringing to press his advantage for promotion and authority. He had everything going for him—intelligence, education, ancestry. It wasn't long before he had climbed to prominence in the ranks of the Jewish religious leadership, and he did so with the blessings of the Romans, who were aware of his citizenship and impressed with his knowledge of their customs. Who better to one day become high priest than a Pharisee who was also a Roman citizen?

The late-second-century apocryphal *Acts of Paul* and *Thecla* describes Saul as a "man small of stature, with bald head and crooked legs ... with eyebrows meeting and nose somewhat hooked."[9] It would seem that what he lacked in height and appearance, even as a youth, he worked hard to make up for in scholarship, determination, and uncompromising pursuit of his goals.

SAUL THE PERSECUTOR

Paul's early ambitions are perhaps best seen in his zeal to wipe out the followers of Jesus. While we have no record that Saul ever encountered

Jesus or heard Him speak, we do know that he violently opposed the early Christian movement. He also seemed to recognize the advantage his zeal would gain him in the eyes of the Jewish leadership. So motivated was he, that Paul rejected the advice of his own teacher, Gamaliel.

Gamaliel had expressed his thoughts about how the followers of Jesus should be dealt with: "Men of Israel, take heed to yourselves what you intend to do regarding these men. For some time ago Theudas rose up, claiming to be somebody. A number of men, about four hundred, joined him. He was slain, and all who obeyed him were scattered and came to nothing. After this man, Judas of Galilee rose up in the days of the census, and drew away many people after him. He also perished, and all who obeyed him were dispersed. And now I say to you, keep away from these men and let them alone; for if this plan or this work is of men, it will come to nothing; but if it is of God, you cannot overthrow it—lest you even be found to fight against God" (Acts 5:35-39 NKJV).

Saul was religious to a fault. While he refused to shed a drop of Stephen's blood at his stoning recorded in Acts 7, he was more than willing to stand by and hold the coats of those who took part—carrying out his purpose while holding carefully to the letter of the Law. He did not have the same problem with throwing believers in prison however, nor was he averse to traveling far and wide to stamp out this new sect.

In a short time, he had built a reputation as a fierce persecutor of Jesus' followers. It is easy to understand why Saul did not see Jesus as the Messiah. For him religion was a means to an end, a path to his goals of leadership and wealth, and his Messiah would be a conqueror before whom all other nations of the world would bow. This man who died on the Cross without a fight was certainly not worthy of his allegiance.

Still … all of that changed in a single day.

ON THE ROAD TO DAMASCUS

Saul was on the road to Damascus with letters from the high priest blessing his mission to extradite the Christians from Damascus to jail cells in Jerusalem. Just as they were approaching Damascus, a light from heaven shown down on Saul, blinding him and throwing him to the ground. The great persecutor then heard the voice of Jesus: "Saul, Saul, why are you persecuting Me?" (Acts 9:4 NKJV).[10]

In an instant, Saul realized that the defeated, executed Jesus was no misguided rebel, but the living Messiah. When the encounter was over, Saul rose to his feet and was led to Damascus. No, the others assured him. They had heard a sound but seen nothing.

Saul was no longer interested in capturing Christians and returning them to Jerusalem. Instead, he sat alone, blinded, refusing food and drink. There he remained until God sent a disciple named Ananias to pray for him. Three days after his encounter with Jesus Christ on the road to Damascus, the scales fell from his eyes and he could see again. Acts 9:18-19 (NIV) says: "[Saul] got up and was baptized, and after taking some food, he regained his strength."

Soon after, Saul began sharing his testimony and preaching in the synagogues of Damascus, loudly proclaiming Jesus as the Messiah. Saul stayed in Damascus for some time, learning all he could from the disciples there and growing strong in his faith. Scholars estimate that Saul's conversion took place in 34 AD (at most four or five years after the Crucifixion and Resurrection of Jesus Christ).

According to his letter to the Galatians and Luke's history of the early church in the book of Acts, Paul spent the next three years of his life studying and teaching in Arabia and Damascus. It seems likely that he spent this time searching the Old Testament Scriptures and prophecies about the Messiah to show how Jesus had fulfilled them, as well as studying the life and teachings of Jesus from the reports of others.

Near the end of these three years, he returned to Damascus where "Saul kept increasing in strength and confounding the Jews who lived at Damascus by proving that this Jesus is the Christ [Messiah]" (Acts 9:22 NASB [insert added]). It was not long before these "confounded" Jews plotted to do away with Saul to shut him up, and he fled for his life. In order to escape, he was lowered in a basket through a hole in the city wall by night to avoid those waiting at the gates to kill him.

From Damascus, Saul returned to Jerusalem. His first attempts to meet with church leaders there were frustrated by his reputation as a persecutor and the suspicion that Saul was trying to trap them only in order to deliver them to the Jewish religious leaders. No one would agree to meet with him except Barnabas, who eventually reconciled Saul with the others and took Saul to meet with Peter and James.

Saul began again to boldly proclaim Jesus as the Messiah throughout Jerusalem, which motivated another plot to kill him—this time by a group of Greek Jews. When the Christian brothers heard of it, they smuggled Saul out of Jerusalem to Caesarea and sent him off to Tarsus. According to Galatians 2:1, fourteen years would pass before Saul would return to Jerusalem.

BARNABAS AND SAUL IN ANTIOCH

In the meantime, other believers were also leaving Jerusalem and Israel because of these persecutions, and one such group traveled to Antioch. Because of their preaching, a revival broke out there among both the Jews and the Gentiles (this was soon after God had shown Peter that the Gospel was for both the Jews and the Gentiles.) (See Acts 10:1–11:18.) When the church leaders in Jerusalem heard about this revival, they sent Barnabas to investigate.

Upon his arrival, Barnabas found a great hunger for more teaching about Jesus—too much for one man to handle. He went to Tarsus, enlisted the help of Saul, and turned with him to Antioch to continue encouraging the new believers "that with purpose of heart they should continue with the Lord" (Acts 11:23 NKJV). It seems that it was in Antioch that God first laid a burden for the Gentiles on Saul's heart, as it was also in Antioch that for the first time followers of Jesus were called Christians. (See Acts 11:26.) Christianity was just being understood as a message of salvation for all humankind.

THE FIRST MISSIONARY JOURNEY

During a prayer meeting of the leaders of the church in Antioch, the Holy Spirit set Barnabas and Saul apart for a new work to which God was calling them. (See Acts 13:1-3.) As a result, Barnabas, Saul, and Barnabas' nephew, John Mark (probably with others not mentioned) embarked on what was to become known as Saul's first missionary journey. To begin this, they traveled to the coastal town of Seleucia and then by boat to Salamis on the island of Cyprus.

Barnabas and Saul took the message of Jesus the Messiah to the synagogues throughout Cyprus starting in Salamis all the way to Paphos. In Paphos, the Roman proconsul called Barnabas and Saul before him so that he could hear what they were teaching, but a sorcerer named Elymas opposed them and sought to discredit their message before the proconsul. At this, Saul, filled with the Holy Spirit, rose up and rebuked Elymas, after which the Holy Spirit struck Elymas blind. At this the proconsul believed.

Two other significant things happened sometime around these events in Paphos. The first was that Saul stopped being called by the Aramaic form of his name—"Saul"—in favor of the Roman form—"Paul." The second was that before this encounter Saul was always listed behind Barnabas, indicating he was following Barnabas' leadership wherever they traveled. But, Acts 13:13 proclaims the group as "Paul and his company." It appears that in Paphos Paul took over the leadership of the delegation as Barnabas and the others recognized what God was doing through him.

From Paphos, they traveled by boat to the province of Pamphylia (in what is today the nation of Turkey) and the cities of Attalia and Perga (where John Mark—later author of the gospel of Mark—"deserted" them), then on to the province of Pisidia and the city of Antioch (not to be confused with the Antioch in Syria). It was in Pisidian Antioch that Paul more fully recognized it was God's calling on his life to take the Gospel to the Gentiles. Before when he went to a new place, he would first preach Jesus in the synagogues. But now, he found that unnecessary. Instead, he preached the Gospel wherever he could muster a crowd. Signs, wonders, and healings continued as they went from town to town.

Paul's message of God's salvation provided through Jesus Christ met resistance wherever Paul preached it. In Pisidian Antioch, Jews who did not receive Paul's teachings rose up against him and drove him on to the towns of Iconium and then Lystra in the province of Lycaonia. Eventually his persecutors followed him to Lystra where they mustered a mob, stoned him, dragged him out of town, and left him for dead. (See Acts 14:19-20; 2 Corinthians 11:25.) The Great Persecutor had become the "Persecuted."

Paul's mission on earth was far from over, however, and God raised him up to continue on to Derbe. After teaching there, he returned through Lystra, Iconium, and Pisidian Antioch to strengthen the new brethren in these regions, and later returned by boat to Antioch of Syria.

PAUL RETURNS TO JERUSALEM

In Paul and Barnabas' absence, a dispute had arisen in the church of Antioch about what responsibilities Christians had to Jewish law. Based on what he had learned in prayer and meditation on the scriptures, as well as what he had seen God do in his travels, Paul knew Jesus had fulfilled the purpose of the law, and now salvation was found through faith in Jesus Christ alone. Because of this, he felt compelled to return to Jerusalem in an official capacity, testify of what God was doing among the Gentiles, and establish with the leaders of the church that being circumcised and conforming to Jewish Law was unnecessary to receive salvation.

Thus Paul's "official"[11] return to Jerusalem was to meet with Church leaders in an effort to clarify these points. Peter and James supported Paul's doctrine of salvation through faith in the "church council" reported in Acts 15 (which probably took place circa AD 50). But, it would take time for the Church to fully deliver itself from the bonds of legalism and sectarianism. After all, these were deeply ingrained parts of their Jewish heritage.

Peter and James suggested that new Gentile believers should be required to follow only certain parts of the law such as abstaining "from things polluted by idols, from sexual immorality, from things strangled, and from blood" (Acts 15:20 NKJV). Yet Paul reports in his letter to the Galatians that "They desired only that we should remember the poor, the very thing which I also was eager to do" (Galatians 2:10 NKJV). This is perhaps Paul's first small step toward the revelation that love alone was the fulfillment of the whole law, as he would write later to the Roman believers. (See Romans 13:10.)

Despite Paul's best efforts, however, the controversy continued. Sometime later, Paul was compelled to rebuke Peter in Antioch for refusing to eat with Gentile believers. Paul suggested that Peter was simply afraid of the legalists who were contradicting Paul's teachings and saying that new male believers needed to be circumcised before they could be saved and Jews should not break bread with Gentiles. (See Galatians 2:11-21.)

PAUL'S SECOND MISSIONARY JOURNEY

After this meeting in Jerusalem, Paul and Barnabas returned to teach and preach in Antioch of Syria. After some months there, Paul again felt prompted to take the Gospel westward, but he and Barnabas had a falling out over who should accompany them. Barnabas wanted to take John Mark along, but Paul, still bothered by John Mark's desertion, would not agree. Instead, Paul promoted the idea of taking Silas. The disagreement caused the two missionaries to go their separate ways— Barnabas and John Mark set sail for Cyprus, never to be mentioned in the book of Acts again. Church history holds that John Mark eventually left to travel with Peter, from whose sermons he wrote the gospel of

Mark, while Barnabas, who was originally from Cyprus, was eventually martyred there. Paul and Silas traveled overland through Tarsus to revisit Derbe, Lystra, Iconium, and Pisidian Antioch. Along the way, Timothy joined them.

On this second journey, Paul traveled on through Galatia, but was forbidden by the Holy Spirit to continue eastward, so he and his companions turned north. When they reached Mysia, the Holy Spirit again changed their direction. Instead of continuing north into the province of Bithynia, they headed west and eventually wound up in Troas on the western coast of Asia Minor. Here Paul had a vision:

> There stood a man of Macedonia, and prayed him, saying, Come over into Macedonia, and help us. And after he had seen the vision, immediately we endeavored to go into Macedonia, assuredly gathering that the Lord had called us for to preach the gospel unto them.

—Acts 16:9-10

From Troas Paul and company took a ship to Neapolis and from there traveled to Philippi, where a church was started in the household of a businesswoman named Lydia. After this, Paul delivered a young slave girl of a spirit of divination, which angered her masters who had been profiting from her fortune-telling. They went to the authorities with their complaints and had Paul and Silas arrested, beaten, and thrown into prison. That night they sang praises and thanksgivings to God because they had been counted worthy enough to suffer persecution for doing good. Eventually they were interrupted when an earthquake shook the jail until the doors of the cells sprang open. As a result of this miracle, the jailer and his family were saved.

From Philippi, the two traveled to Thessalonica, where Paul again preached and saw many come to Christ. Yet they were forced to flee by those who were jealous of their faith. From Thessalonica, they went to Berea, of whom the book of Acts tells us:

> These were more noble than those in Thessalonica, in that they received the word with all readiness of mind, and searched the scriptures daily, whether those things were so. Therefore many of them believed.
>
> —*Acts 17:11-12*

When those who had persecuted them in Thessolonica heard what was happening in Berea, they went to drive Paul out of there as well. But Paul was able to leave Silas and Timothy to further encourage and establish the believers, and he traveled by ship to Athens, where the Word of God met with little response. Paul then traveled to Corinth where he spent the next year and a half (circa AD 53-55) establishing a church beginning in the home of Aquila and Priscilla, a Jew and his wife who had moved to Corinth when Emperor Claudius expelled all of the Jews from Rome. Eventually Silas and Timothy joined him in Corinth with good news of what was happening in Macedonia. Paul was jubilant to hear of the work the Thessalonians were doing and sent them his first letter. Though there is some scholarly debate on this point, it also seems likely Paul wrote his letter to the Galatians during this stay in Corinth. though some suggest an earlier writing. It is believed Paul's second letter to Thessalonica was also written during this time in Corinth.

From Corinth, Paul traveled by boat with Priscilla and Aquila and landed in Ephesus. Here Paul forcefully preached in the synagogues that Jesus was the Messiah. Some in Ephesus asked that he remain there and teach them further, but he felt compelled to move on. Leaving Priscilla and Aquila to minister in Ephesus, Paul departed for Caesarea, returned to Jerusalem, and then eventually went back to Antioch of Syria.

PAUL'S THIRD MISSIONARY JOURNEY

Shortly after his return to Antioch, Paul set out again to strengthen the churches he'd planted in Galatia and Phrygia before returning to Ephesus for two years "so that all they which dwelt in Asia [Minor] heard the word of the Lord Jesus, both Jews and Greeks" (Acts 19:10 [insert added]). It was during this time (circa AD 57-60) that handkerchiefs and aprons were sent to Paul so that he could lay his hands on them and pray. So potent were his prayers that God's healing and delivering power traveled throughout the region. It was a busy time, but Paul found time to write to the Corinthians while he was there.

The impact of the Gospel in Ephesus was so great that many in the occult gathered their magic books and burned them in a public display of their allegiance to Christ (the value of these books was estimated at 50,000 pieces of silver). In another incident, a group of Jewish exorcists were beaten and left naked by a demonic spirit when they tried to cast him out in the name of "the Jesus whom Paul preaches" (Acts 19:13 NKJV). Finally so many were coming to Christ that those who made their living by producing and selling idols were being driven out of business. As a result, they formed a mob in protest of the growing Christian population and took the issue before the city officials who found that no crimes had been committed and dispersed the crowd.

Shortly before these riots, Paul sent Timothy and Erastus back through Macedonia to Corinth to prepare the way for his return. Paul later followed, exhorting the believers in every town along the way. (See Acts 20:1-3.) Many think that Paul wrote his second letter to the Corinthians while in Macedonia on the way back to Athens and Corinth. When he arrived again in Corinth, he spent three months there. While he felt compelled to continue on to Rome at the end of that time, he felt he should first return to Jerusalem. Paul wrote his letter to the Romans during this time in the hope that he would soon see the believers there.

Paul then retraced his steps through Macedonia to Philippi from where he sailed to Troas and spent a week. During this stay, on the first day of the week, he went to eat with a group of disciples. Since he was planning to leave the next day, the group kept him teaching until midnight. A youth named Eutychus, who had been sitting in a windowsill listening, fell asleep and tumbled three floors to his death. When Paul saw what had happened, he went to the young man, embraced him, and the youth's spirit returned to him.

Paul's next stop was Mitylene (the largest city on the Greek island of Lesvos), then on to Chios, Trogyllium, and Miletus. In Miletus, the Ephesians elders went to him in answer to his summons, and he told them of the bonds that he knew by the Spirit awaited him in Jerusalem. Paul said his good-byes—certain that he would never travel that way again—and exhorted them to remain strong in the Gospel, acting as shepherds, protecting the church against false prophets and persecutions that would come.

Paul sailed from there for Patara, then Tyre—where he was again warned through the Spirit that bonds awaited him in Jerusalem—then on to Caesarea. In Caesarea Paul stayed in the home of Philip the Evangelist and his four daughters who were all prophetesses. There Agabus went to him and warned Paul that he would be arrested and imprisoned if he continued on to Jerusalem. But Paul was undeterred. When others wept for him and urged him not to go, he only answered:

> "What do you mean by weeping and breaking my heart? For I am ready not only to be bound, but also to die at Jerusalem for the name of the Lord Jesus."
>
> —*Acts 21:13* NKJV

Some days after that, Paul returned overland to Jerusalem.

PAUL'S FINAL VISIT IN JERUSALEM

Paul arrived in Jerusalem for the last time around AD 60. Those in the church—among them James and some of the other elders—welcomed Paul warmly and glorified God when Paul told them of his travels and all who were coming to the Lord in Asia Minor, Macedonia, and Greece. When he was done, they warned Paul of the controversy that his ministry was causing among the legalistic Jews. In the hope of appeasing these Jews, James and the others urged Paul to join a group of four who were going to vow a vow to purify themselves. As was the custom, they would shave their heads, go to the temple to pray for seven days, and in the end offer sacrifices of cleansing. They hoped this would show those in Jerusalem that Paul still honored the Law.

However, as the seven days grew to an end, a group of the Jews who had opposed Paul in Asia Minor stirred up the Jews of Jerusalem:

"Men of Israel, help! This is the man who teaches all
men everywhere against the people, the law, and this
place; and furthermore he also brought Greeks into
the temple and has defiled this holy place."

—*Acts 21:28* NKJV

As a result, a mob seized Paul, intending to take him out of the
temple and kill him. Their efforts were thwarted by Roman soldiers
who put Paul in chains and demanded to know who he was and what
he had done. When no one could give a satisfactory answer, the
soldiers assumed Paul was an Egyptian who had recently stirred up an
insurrection involving four thousand men. They knew nothing different until Paul spoke to them in Greek and asked them to quiet the
crowd so he could address them.

Paul's desire was to defend himself by telling his testimony and what
God had done through him. When the crowd heard him speak in
Hebrew, they quieted. Paul told them that he had once persecuted
those in the way of Jesus. He also spoke of his conversion on the road
to Damascus, how the Lord had healed his blindness, and finally told
them that God had called him to take the Gospel to the Gentiles.

At this, the crowd erupted in renewed anger. They cried out, throwing off their cloaks and tossing dust in the air. Soon they were calling
for Paul to be slain as a blasphemer. To keep the peace, the Romans
hustled Paul back to their barracks where they planned to scourge him
until they learned why he had so angered the mob. They had not
understood what he had said in Hebrew. At this, Paul asked them
about the legality of beating a Roman citizen, and then the commander
of the cohort stopped the preparations to scourge Paul. The next day
he had Paul released, but not before he called together the chief priests

and Counsel of the Jews so that he could get to the bottom of the matter and find out why they were trying to kill Paul.

Paul again spoke boldly in defense of the truth. But again the chief priests and Jewish leaders were angered. For his own protection, the soldiers removed Paul and placed him in custody. The next night, Jesus appeared to Paul and told him:

> "Be of good cheer, Paul; for as you have testified for Me
> in Jerusalem, so you must also bear witness at Rome."
> —*Acts 23:11* NKJV

Meanwhile, a conspiracy was formed against Paul. More than forty individuals vowed they would neither eat nor drink until he was dead. They planned to call for Paul to be brought to public trial and then take the opportunity to assassinate him. Paul's nephew heard about the planned ambush, however, and warned Paul and the centurion commander. Paul was taken by military guard out of Jerusalem that very night and presented to the Roman governor Felix in Caesarea.

This gave Paul the opportunity to present the Gospel to Felix as he testified in his own defense. Paul remained in prison there for two years, being taken before Felix often to discuss matters of faith and the ways of righteousness. But Felix was more interested in Paul bribing his way out than in coming to the truth, and in the end, when Felix was replaced as governor by Porcius Festus, he left Paul in prison as a favor to the Jews.

When Festus arrived in Israel, Jewish leaders again accused Paul of every crime they could think of, though they could prove none of them. Paul took the opportunity to defend the faith before Festus. When Festus suggested that Paul should return to Jerusalem to be tried, he responded by saying:

"I stand at Caesar's judgment seat, where I ought to be judged. To the Jews I have done no wrong, as you very well know. For if I am an offender, or have committed anything deserving of death, I do not object to dying; but if there is nothing in these things of which these men accuse me, no one can deliver me to them. I appeal to Caesar."

—*Acts 25:10-11* NKJV

When Festus had conferred with his council, he agreed: "You have appealed to Caesar? To Caesar you shall go!" (Acts 25:12 NKJV)

Before Paul was to be taken to Rome, King Agrippa and his sister, Bernice, arrived for a visit, and after Festus told them of Paul's case, Agrippa asked if he might hear Paul speak for himself. The following day Paul was again permitted to present an explanation for his faith in Jesus Christ before Festus, King Agrippa, Bernice, local military commanders, and other prominent leaders of the region. Paul spoke eloquently while presenting his case, and in the end, as Festus accused him of being mad because he proclaimed Jesus the first to be risen among the dead, Agrippa admitted, "You almost persuade me to become a Christian" (Acts 26:28 NKJV). Others suggested that Paul was innocent and should be released. However, because he had appealed to Caesar, he would still have to be sent to Rome to be judged.

PAUL'S JOURNEY TO ROME

Paul and some other prisoners were delivered over to an Augustan centurion named Julius and put on an Adramyttiam ship headed west. Luke and Aristarchus, a Macedonian from Thessalonica, traveled with

Paul and the others. Their first stop was in Sidon, where Paul was allowed to go ashore and receive care from friends. From there the ship sailed north of Cyprus and landed in Myra in Lycia. In Myra, Julius found an Alexandrian ship headed for Rome and put them aboard it.

When they put to sea again, the winds were against them, so they turned south to travel around Crete. They sailed with some difficulties and next put in at Fair Havens on the southern side of Crete. Because the seas were unfavorable for travel, they were forced to stay there for some time. When impatience caused them to sail anyway, Paul warned, "Men, I perceive that this voyage will end with disaster and much loss, not only of the cargo and ship, but also our lives" (Acts 27:10 NKJV). However, Julius listened more to the helmsman and owner of the ship, and they decided to set out for Phoenix, on the northwest side of Crete—a place that offered a better harbor in which to winter.

A short time later, receiving a favorably moderate southern wind, they set out trying to keep near the shore. However, not long into the trip they hit a violent southeastern wind called the Euroclydon, which kicked up the waves and drove the ship out to sea. The next day only brought a more violent storm, and, fearing they would be driven south onto the shallows of Syrtis in northern Africa, they put down the sea anchor to hold their course steadier, secured the rudder with ropes, and helplessly let the ship be driven along before the winds. The next day they began jettisoning the ship's cargo in the hope of remaining afloat, and the following day threw the ship's tackle overboard with their own hands. For fourteen days they saw neither the sun nor the stars. They might all have given up hope if Paul had not stood forward and proclaimed:

> "Men, you should have listened to me, and not have
> sailed from Crete and incurred this disaster and loss.

And now I urge you to take heart, for there will be no
loss of life among you, but only of the ship. For there
stood by me this night an angel of the God to whom I
belong and whom I serve, saying, 'Do not be afraid,
Paul; you must be brought before Caesar; and indeed
God has granted you all those who sail with you.'
Therefore take heart, men, for I believe God that it
will be just as it was told me. However, we must run
aground on a certain island."

—Acts 27:21-26 NKJV

On the fourteenth night of the storm, around midnight, the sailors
felt that they might be approaching shore, so they let down soundings
to find the waters growing increasingly shallow. Fearing they would be
run aground on some unseen and rugged coastline, they put out four
anchors in the stern of the ship and hoped for daybreak. A group of the
sailors, hoping to escape with their lives, decided to tell the others they
were putting out one of the ship's boats to lay anchors from the bow.
Their intention was to slip undetected from the ship and desert the
others. Paul warned Julius of their plan, however, and because they
could not sail the ship without these men, he cut the lines to the boat
and let it float away before they could board it.

At this point, Paul urged them all to eat the remainder of the provi-
sions so that they might have some strength for the struggle to reach
shore that was about to come. He also promised each of them that not
a hair on their heads would be harmed. Then he took bread, broke it,
gave thanks for it, and ate. When the others had eaten, they threw the
remaining wheat overboard in a final attempt to keep the ship afloat.

As dawn lightened the sky, they barely made out what looked to be a beach. They cut the anchors loose, cut the ropes that had held the rudder steady in the high winds, hoisted the sails, and resolved to drive the ship onto the sand. Some short distance from shore, however, they stuck solidly in a reef, and the wind and waves were so violent that they began to pound the back part of the ship into pieces. Fearing their escape, some of the soldiers decided to kill the prisoners and make for shore. However, Julius prevented them, wanting to protect Paul for all he had done. Julius then commanded that all who could swim should jump overboard and make for shore while the rest followed on whatever they could find that floated. Just as Paul had promised, the entire 276 souls on board the ship made it safely to shore.

The group had landed on the island of Malta, and those living there showed them great kindness. To help them dry, they started a fire. When Paul picked up a bundle of sticks to add to the fire, a viper came out of it and fastened itself onto his hand. The islanders suspected that he was a murderer and justice would not allow him to live even though he had just been saved from the sea. However, Paul merely shook the snake off into the fire. When his hand didn't swell and he didn't grow sick from the bite, the islanders began to regard him as a god. Then when Paul laid hands on and prayed for a local village leader's father and the man was healed, all of the sick on the island came to him asking for prayer.

Three months later, Paul set sail for Rome on a ship that had wintered on the island. The locals supplied them with everything they needed for the voyage. From there they sailed north and put in at Syracuse on the island of Sicily, then Rhegium, Puteoli, and on to Rome overland. When believers in Rome heard they were coming, they went as far south as Three Taverns and Appius to meet them. Paul and his companions rejoiced at their coming.

PAUL'S FINAL YEARS

Upon arriving in Rome (sometime around AD 60), Paul was allowed to find his own residence where he remained under Roman guard. Here he again proclaimed Jesus as the Messiah to the Jewish leaders and all who would come to hear. When the Jews in Rome refused to believe, Paul rebuked them:

> "Let it be known to you that the salvation of God has been sent to the Gentiles, and they will hear it!"
> —*Acts 28:28* NKJV

The Jews departed, arguing among themselves.

For the next two years, Paul remained in his rented house welcoming all who came to him and freely preaching the kingdom of God and Jesus the Messiah. It is believed that it was during this time he wrote his prison epistles to the Ephesians, Philippians, Colossians, and Philemon, as well as the first two of his pastoral epistles to Timothy and Titus.

Since this is where the book of Acts ends, there is much conjecture as to what happened in the rest of Paul's life. A common belief is that Paul had two Roman imprisonments. It is believed that Paul was left pretty much to himself except for a guard during his first imprisonment. The second was spent in an actual prison.

Acts indicates that Paul's first imprisonment ended two years after his arrival in Rome—which would have been sometime around AD 62.

Many believe that Paul did further missionary work for the next three years, traveling west perhaps as far as the Spanish Peninsula, but was then imprisoned again upon his return. It was during this last imprisonment that Paul wrote his final epistle preserved in our modern Bible, the letter of 2 Timothy. In it, Paul bid his farewell:

> I am already being poured out as a drink offering, and the time of my departure is at hand. I have fought the good fight, I have finished the race, I have kept the faith. Finally, there is laid up for me the crown of righteousness, which the Lord, the righteous Judge, will give to me on that Day, and not to me only but also to all who have loved His appearing.
>
> —*2 Timothy 4:6-8* NKJV

Church history tells us that Paul was beheaded in Rome sometime around AD 66. St. Paul's Cathedral, which still stands in the modern Italian city of Rome, was built to commemorate the location were Paul finally finished his race and went home to his reward.

APPENDIX

All of the Prayers of Paul

In the order they appear in the New Testament

Topic	Passage Location
Paul's prayer to be saved	Acts 9:5-6
	(repeated in Acts 22:8,10; 26:15)
"That I might come unto you"	Romans 1:9-10
A Prayer that Israel Be Saved	Romans 10:1
A Prayer for Unity	Romans 15:5-6
A Prayer for Hope	Romans 15:13
"Now the God of peace be with you all. Amen."	Romans 15:33
A Benediction—"Grace be with you"	Romans 16:20, 24
A Prayer of Praise and Thanksgiving	Romans 16:25-27
A Prayer of Praise and Thanksgiving	1 Corinthians 1:4-9
A Benediction—"Grace be with you"	1 Corinthians 16:23-24
A Prayer of Praise and Thanksgiving— "Blessed be the God of all comfort"	2 Corinthians 1:3-5
A Prayer of Praise and Thanksgiving	2 Corinthians 2:14
A Prayer of Praise and Thanksgiving	2 Corinthians 9:15
"I pray to God that you do no evil"	2 Corinthians 13:7-9
A Benediction—His Presence be with you	2 Corinthians 13:14
A Benediction—"Grace be with you"	Galatians 1:3-5
A Benediction—"Grace be with you"	Galatians 6:18
A Prayer for Revelation	Ephesians 1:15-23
A Prayer for Spiritual Strength	Ephesians 3:14-21
A Benediction—Peace, Love with Faith, and Grace be with you	Ephesians 6:23-24
A Prayer for Guidance	Philippians 1:9-11

By Category and Topic

Topic	Passage Location
Power Prayers	
A Prayer for Abounding Love	1 Thessalonians 3:11-13

A Prayer for Effective Faith	Philemon 4-6
A Prayer for Fulfilling Purpose	2 Thessalonians 1:11-12
A Prayer for Guidance	Philippians 1:9-11
A Prayer for Hope	Romans 15:13
A Prayer for Patience	2 Thessalonians 3:5
A Prayer for Peace	2 Thessalonians 3:16
A Prayer for Revelation	Ephesians 1:15-23
A Prayer for Right Priorities	Colossians 1:9-12
A Prayer for Spiritual Strength	Ephesians 3:14-21
A Prayer for Steadfastness in the Truth	2 Thessalonians 2:16-17
A Prayer for Total Sanctification	1 Thessalonians 5:23-24
A Prayer for Unity	Romans 15:5-6

Minor Prayers

Paul's prayer to be saved	Acts 9:5-6
	(repeated in Acts 22:8,10; 26:15)
"That I might come unto you"	Romans 1:9-10
A Prayer that Israel Be Saved	Romans 10:1
"Now the God of peace be with you all. Amen."	Romans 15:33
"I pray to God that you do no evil"	2 Corinthians 13:7-9
A Prayer for Justice	2 Timothy 4:14-16
A Prayer for Onesiphorus	2 Timothy 1:16-18

Prayers of Praise and Thanksgiving

A Prayer of Praise and Thanksgiving	Romans 16:25-27
A Prayer of Praise and Thanksgiving	1 Corinthians 1:4-9
A Prayer of Praise and Thanksgiving— "Blessed be the God of all comfort"	2 Corinthians 1:3-5
A Prayer of Praise and Thanksgiving	2 Corinthians 2:14
A Prayer of Praise and Thanksgiving	2 Corinthians 9:15
A Prayer of Praise and Thanksgiving	1 Thessalonians 1:2-4
A Prayer of Praise and Thanksgiving	1 Thessalonians 2:13

A Prayer of Praise and Thanksgiving— "To God be the glory"	Philippians 4:20
A Prayer of Praise and Thanksgiving	1 Timothy 1:12
A Prayer of Praise and Thanksgiving	1 Timothy 1:17
A Prayer of Praise and Thanksgiving	1 Timothy 6:15-16
A Prayer of Praise and Thanksgiving	2 Timothy 1:3
A Prayer of Praise and Thanksgiving	2 Timothy 4:18

Benedictions

A Benediction—"Grace be with you"	Romans 16:20, 24
A Benediction—"Grace be with you"	1 Corinthians 16:23-24
A Benediction—His Presence be with you	2 Corinthians 13:14
A Benediction—"Grace be with you"	Galatians 1:3-5
A Benediction—"Grace be with you"	Galatians 6:18
A Benediction—Peace, Love with Faith, and Grace be with you	Ephesians 6:23-24
A Benediction—"Grace be with you"	Philippians 4:23
A Benediction—"Grace be with you"	Colossians 4:18
A Benediction—"Grace be with you"	1 Thessalonians 5:28
A Benediction—"Grace be with you"	2 Thessalonians 3:18
A Benediction—"Grace be with you"	1 Timothy 6:21
A Benediction—"Grace be with you"	2 Timothy 4:22
A Benediction—"Grace be with you"	Titus 3:15
A Benediction—"Grace be with you"	Philemon 25

ENDNOTES

1 (p. 229) David B. Barrett and Todd M. Johnson, *World Christian Trends AD 30–AD 2200: Interpreting the Annual Christian Megacensus* (Pasadena: William Carey Library, 2001).

2 ("pray, prayer") W.E. Vine, Merrill F. Unger, and William White. *Vine's Complete Expository Dictionary of Old and New Testament Words* (Nashville: Thomas Nelson, 1996).

3 ("intercession") Merriam-Webster, Inc. *Merriam-Webster's Collegiate Dictionary.* 10th ed. (Springfield, Mass.: Merriam-Webster, 1996).

4 ("hope") Ibid.

5 ("hope") Vine, et. al., *Vine's Complete Expository Dictionary of Old and New Testament Words.*

6 A quick search on the Internet will pull up several articles discussing these theories; however, one good article on the topic is Tom Paulu's "OMSI invites you to do the 'unsinkable' TITANIC," on-line at: http://www.tdn.com/articles/2004/06/03/this_day/news01.txt. Created: 3 June 2004. Accessed: 3 March 2005.

7 (p. 63) Richard Wurmbrand, *Tortured for Christ, 30th Anniversary Edition* (Bartlesville, OK: Living Sacrifice Book Company, 1998).

8 ("shalom") James Strong, *The Exhaustive Concordance of the Bible: Showing Every Word of the Text of the Common English Version of the Canonical Books, and Every Occurrence of Each Word in Regular Order,* electronic edition (Ontario: Woodside Bible Fellowship, 1996).

9 ("Paul") Paul J. Achtemeier, *Harper's Bible Dictionary.* 1st ed. (San Francisco: Harper & Row Society of Biblical Literature, 1985).

10 Saul's conversion experience is actually told three times: Acts 9:1-19; 22:3-16; 26:4-18.

11 According to the book of Acts, Barnabas and Paul did return to Jerusalem one other time shortly before their missionary journey to deliver an offering for famine relief to the church in Jerusalem (probably around AD 37). Paul doesn't mention that particular trip in the retelling of his testimony in his letter to the Galatians.

PRAYER OF SALVATION

God loves you—no matter who you are, no matter what your past. God loves you so much that He gave His one and only begotten Son for you. The Bible tells us that "…whoever believes in him shall not perish but have eternal life" (John 3:16 NIV). Jesus laid down His life and rose again so that we could spend eternity with Him in heaven and experience His absolute best on earth. If you would like to receive Jesus into your life, say the following prayer out loud and mean it from your heart.

Heavenly Father, I come to You admitting that I am a sinner. Right now, I choose to turn away from sin, and I ask You to cleanse me of all unrighteousness. I believe that Your Son, Jesus, died on the cross to take away my sins. I also believe that He rose again from the dead so that I might be forgiven of my sins and made righteous through faith in Him. I call upon the name of Jesus Christ to be the Savior and Lord of my life. Jesus, I choose to follow You and ask that You fill me with the power of the Holy Spirit. I declare that right now I am a child of God. I am free from sin and full of the righteousness of God. I am saved in Jesus' name. Amen.

If you prayed this prayer to receive Jesus Christ as your Savior for the first time, please contact us on the web at **www.harrisonhouse.com** to receive a free book.

Or you may write to us at

Harrison House
P.O. Box 35035
Tulsa, Oklahoma 74153

ABOUT THE AUTHORS

David Bordon has worked in the publishing industry for 18 years. He was the executive vice-president and publisher of Honor Books, a leading inspirational publisher, until 2002 when he launched out to start his own product development and packaging firm that creates book products for publishers. He loves books, sports, the outdoors, and camping. He lives in Tulsa, Oklahoma, with his wife, Rayne', the love of his life for over 26 years.

Rick Killian was the developmental editor on the platinum-selling book by dc Talk and The Voice of the Martyrs, *Jesus Freaks,* as well as the ghostwriter for *Jesus Freaks II* and more recently Michael D. Evan's New York Times bestseller *The American Prophecies.* Other books he has collaborated on include *The Storehouse Principle* by Al Jandl and Van Crouch, *William and Catherine: A New Biography* by Trevor Yaxley, Dr. Reginald Cherry's *God's Pathway to Healing* series, and *The Unanswered Prayers of Jesus* by Michael D. Evans.

Rick and his wife, Melissa, operate Killian Creative, a freelance writing and consulting firm in Boulder, Colorado. They have two children. For more information you can visit their website at www.KillianCreative.com.

www.harrisonhouse.com

Fast. Easy. Convenient!

- ◆ New Book Information
- ◆ Look Inside the Book
- ◆ Press Releases
- ◆ Bestsellers

- ◆ Free E-News
- ◆ Author Biographies
- ◆ Upcoming Books
- ◆ Share Your Testimony

For the latest in book news and author information, please visit us on the Web at www.harrisonhouse.com. Get up-to-date pictures and details on all our powerful and life-changing products. Sign up for our e-mail newsletter, *Friends of the House,* and receive free monthly information on our authors and products including testimonials, author announcements, and more!

Harrison House—
Books That Bring Hope, Books That Bring Change

THE HARRISON HOUSE VISION

Proclaiming the truth and the power
Of the Gospel of Jesus Christ
With excellence;

Challenging Christians to
Live victoriously,
Grow spiritually,
Know God intimately.